# COURAGEOUS KATE

# COURAGEOUS KATE

## A DAUGHTER OF THE AMERICAN REVOLUTION

by **Sheila Ingle**

illustrations by John Ingle

Spartanburg, SC • 2006

ISBN 1-891-885-52-9
Second printing December 2008


Front cover image—James Palmer
Interior illustrations—John Ingle
Book design—Mark Olencki
Project editor—Betsy Teter
Copy editing—Emily L. Smith, Carol Bradof, John Cribb
Fact checking—Tom Moore Craig, George Fields, Melissa Walker

*Illustration on page 135 is made from the only known image of Kate Barry.
It was etched on a broach made when she was middle aged.*

Hub City Writers Project
Post Office Box 8421
Spartanburg, South Carolina 29305
(864) 577-9349 • fax (864) 577-0188 • www.hubcity.org

*For Scott*

# Welcome to Kate's World!

Kate Moore Barry was a courageous woman. She rode Indian trails on horseback all over the Upcountry to warn the settlers of attacks from the British and the Tories during the Revolutionary War. As a scout and spy for her husband Andrew, she helped his militia unit show up in the right place at the right time to protect their families and friends. Neither stormy weather nor enemy horses behind her caused her to falter in her mission to protect her community. Tradition says that on one occasion she crossed the Pacolet River at Hurricane Shoals. The river rose behind her, but she made it up the opposite bank safely. The Tories behind her were stopped as the water rose in front of them.

Because of fearless rides like this, the Upcountry stayed on alert during the war, and few lives were lost. Stories are told about the way she hid food in stumps for the citizen-soldiers who could not get home for provisions. Her life was often in danger as she unselfishly made quick rides up and down the Tyger River.

This biography of Kate covers a span of thirty years and three generations. Many details about her parents' lives and her life are unknown. Because of sketchy information, I took much liberty in adding conversations and actions, so some incidents are more factual in their telling than others. The word "tradition" is used to introduce much of the information I read about Kate's life, and many puzzle pieces are missing.

It was also impossible to include all of the history, customs, or lifestyles of those thirty years in South Carolina history. This book is not a history, and it is a biography of only certain parts of Kate's life. You will notice that it sometimes skips years between the actions from one chapter to another. The house of Charles and Mary Moore on the Tyger River is now called Walnut Grove Plantation, but because history is uncertain about when it picked up that name, I have not used it in this book. For more information about the Scots-Irish settlers during the 1760s and their part in the Revolutionary War, there is a list of references that I used for my research included after the glossary.

Patrick Henry sent out a battle cry with his words, "Give me liberty or give me death!" Kate's parents, Charles and Mary Moore, tamed a wilderness and fought Indians to pass on that liberty to their children. Kate fought as a spy and scout during the Revolutionary War to pass on that freedom to her children.

I fell in love with Kate one day as John and I listened to a guide tell us part of her story on a tour of her parents' home, Walnut Grove Plantation. It was her courage that caught and kept my attention that day. I hope you are both entertained and challenged by Kate's resolve to fight for her family's independence. She left that gift of independence to her children as well as to us and generations to come.

Ship bound for America

# THE JOURNEY ACROSS THE ATLANTIC

"Papa! Papa! I can't stop! Help, Papa!" the six-year-old desperately shouted.

One of the Connor boys had slipped on the deck and was sliding toward the ship's railing. It was John. He was only six and small for his age. His older brothers tried to grab him, but both missed. Then they started to run after their brother.

Master Connor, the boys' father, and fellow passenger Charles Moore stopped talking and immediately started running toward the young boy.

The ship's deck was slippery from the last storm. Some even slipped and stopped themselves by grabbing the ropes around the cargo on the deck.

A sailor caught John's shirt, but the shirt tore. John kept sliding.

"I couldn't hold him!" the sailor hollered.

The terrified boy grabbed for the ropes on the side of the deck.

John shouted again, "Papa, not the water!"

Charles was determined to get to the boy. He

ran ahead of the others and grabbed John by both his arms just before he went over the side.

Master Connor was right behind Charles and took his son from Charles's arms. He looked over his son's head to Charles. He couldn't speak for a moment. Master Connor couldn't stop hugging his crying son.

"Thank you kindly, sir. Thank you kindly," the father whispered. "Your quick-thinking saved my boy. I am in your debt, sir."

All of them remembered the other young boy who fell overboard two weeks before.

No one had been able to save him. That had been a sad day for all the families.

The voyage from Ireland to Pennsylvania took more than two months. Conditions on the ship grew worse daily. The cheese became moldy, but the rats still tried to eat it. The ship's cat was so tired he almost stopped chasing rats. The mothers sometimes had to pick bugs out of the children's food. The salted beef ran out. The hardtack, a firm, dry biscuit, was impossible to chew. Water had to be rationed. Some became so thirsty they drank the salt water. Then they were very sick.

Their merchant ship ran into many storms, and the rolling waves and wind tore some of the sails. Every storm was scary. Most of the children cried. The adults prayed.

Twenty-two-year-old Charles Moore traveled by himself. He had left family and friends in Ireland. Charles was a curious man who never missed an opportunity to learn something. This was his first ocean voyage, and he asked the captain and sailors many questions.

Once he persuaded the captain to let him climb the rigging. He wanted to see beyond the horizon. He lost his balance a couple of times, but Charles wouldn't give up. When he finally reached the crow's nest, he saw a school of flying fish skim across the water. Unbelievably, the fish passed the ship. Charles laughed at the sight.

For a couple of hours, he hollered reports to the other passengers of what he saw from his high perch. Finally the captain called him down.

The sailors spoke their own language. One day Charles heard one of the sailors muttering, "Red sky at morning, sailor take warning. Red sky at night, sailor's delight."

Charles asked him, "What are you saying? Does that mean we are in for bad weather again?"

"Just watch the sky," the sailor answered. "You always have to watch the sky."

Before long that same afternoon, the sailors were battening down the ship again. During the worst of that storm, the crew threw cargo and even some food overboard to keep the ship from sinking. It took days to repair the sails before the ship was underway again.

It was dangerous to cross the Atlantic Ocean in the early 1750s. The voyage took at least two months. There were one hundred ninety-four passengers on board the merchant ship. The quarters were cramped, and there was no privacy.

Just like Charles Moore, most of the passengers on this ship were Scots-Irish. It was a long and tiring voyage from Ireland to America, but every adult and child showed courage. The Scots-Irish were brave and determined. Many complained, but none were sorry they had left Ireland.

These families had left a country where they had no civil liberties or religious freedom. None of the men could hold public office in Ireland. Most owned no land and were in debt because of the English king's taxes. Rents on the land kept going up. The men could not make enough money to feed their families and pay the rent. Starvation was a real possibility. They were also ridiculed because of their Presbyterian religion. All these Scots-Irish families were looking forward to a better life in America. There was no future for them in Scotland.

After weeks in a small ship on the Atlantic Ocean, Charles awoke to the sound of shouts from the deck. "Land, ho! Land, ho!" It was not long before the deck was full of excited passengers. There were shouts and tears when they saw the docks of Philadelphia, Pennsylvania, getting closer and closer. Philadelphia was known to all as the City of Brotherly Love. It had the reputation of being a friendly place to live. A Scots-Irish community was already there.

The merchant ship dropped anchor in the Delaware River. One boat after another filled with the passengers to take them from the ship to the dock. Everyone was ready to walk on dry land again. It had been a long three thousand miles.

Charles held his rifle as he waited his turn to board one of the rowboats. He checked to be sure his money bag still had his few shillings. Then it was time. Charles picked up his small trunk that held all he owned. His Bible, copies of *Aesop's Fables* and *Robinson Crusoe*, and his extra powder and shot were in the trunk.

There was also a handkerchief made by his mother, carefully packed in cloth between the books. He joined the others in the next boat.

The rowboat docked on Market Wharf. Charles quickly jumped out. He held his trunk tightly under his arm and started walking. His sea legs immediately slowed him down. He wobbled and almost fell because he could not keep his balance. It was different walking on land again.

Charles never forgot his first sights, smells, and sounds in America. There was the vendor selling roasted oysters from his street cart. The fishy smell reminded Charles of home. Many stood around the cart to buy the steaming oysters.

His eyes followed the spire of Christ Church, and Charles saw seagulls circling above it. The church was unfinished, but it still towered over the rest of the buildings.

A man walked by pushing a wagon full of apples. A child was sitting on the edge of the wagon eating one of those shiny red apples. There was juice running down the child's chin. The boy looked at Charles and smiled. He said, "Would you like an apple, sir?"

apple. Soon that good apple juice was dripping down Charles's chin, too. It was his first American-grown purchase.

Up and down the streets he saw many Conestoga wagons. Some were full of logs.

Others held bales of hay. Many carried baskets of fresh vegetables. They were headed for the market to sell their crops. Dogs barked at the horse-drawn wagons. The horses paid them no mind. Charles followed the wagons.

It was Saturday and market day on High Street in Philadelphia. There were street lamps on the corners that brightened the city at night. Some were lighted already. It was a cloudy day.

Then he noticed the wooden shingles hanging outside most buildings. There were pictures and names on the shingles. Charles recognized the sign for a tavern and headed up the hill. He needed a place to get a meal and spend the night.

He heard different languages spoken by people who were not dressed like he was.

Quakers, with their plain clothes, walked beside the obviously wealthy. Others were in frontier dress, carrying their rifles. Charles saw friendly smiles on those faces. No one frowned at him as if he didn't belong, like they did in Ireland. Many nodded at him as he walked toward the tavern.

He bought a copy of the *Philadelphia Gazette* from a boy standing on the corner.

Charles couldn't wait to read everything about America.

Charles took a deep breath and inhaled the

newness of this country. He began to smile. He was home and excited about the next part of his adventure! He walked into the Green Tree Tavern.

The innkeeper greeted Charles with a smile. "And how can I help you today, sir?"

Elfreth's Alley
Philadelphia

# THE GREAT PHILADELPHIA WAGON ROAD

Charles Moore did not stay in Philadelphia. He traveled with a group of Scots-Irish men who were going back to their homes in Anson County, North Carolina. Years passed in North Carolina, and in 1763 the adventurous Charles was ready to move again.

This time Charles would not travel alone. Charles was married now and had a family. He and his wife, Mary, were moving to South Carolina with their eight children.

"Tell me again about the wagon road, Papa. Did you really camp beside Indians?" questioned four-year-old Thomas. He patted the floor with his foot as he talked.

Thomas could not talk and sit still at the same time.

"Yes, your Grandpa Barry and I were standing guard across the river from our campsite. We had just taken our places for our shift. Next thing we knew, we heard someone snoring. We didn't make a sound after that. We hardly breathed.

"At daylight we heard muffled voices, and then

there was quiet again. We carefully crawled in the direction of the voices and found where several Indians had camped the night before. It was days before we told the women about what happened," his father answered.

"What is the name of that road again?" asked Alice. Alice was the second daughter in the family. She was almost as curious as Thomas.

"I know!" exclaimed Thomas. "It is the Great Philadelphia Wagon Road."

"Thomas," said his mama, "Sing not. Hum not. Wiggle not. Did you forget your table manners?" She stifled a smile as she spoke to her only son.

"No, Mama, I am really trying to sit still today. Papa, I think I could sit still a lot better if you told us again about your journey from way up in Philadelphia to our home here," Thomas pleaded.

Charles looked at Thomas with a twinkle in his eye. "You might be a politician one day, my son. Yes, I will be glad to tell you my story again. It is important that all of you children know about your family's history."

"Papa, are you going to tell us the short story or the long story tonight?" Violet asked. Violet was only a year older than Thomas.

"I think your Papa is going to tell us his short story tonight. It is almost your bedtime," said Mary quietly. Charles winked at his wife and began to speak.

"I woke up my first morning in Philadelphia so excited about being here in America. I didn't know how I was going to make a living or where I was going to live. It really didn't matter to me. I knew I was going to be fine.

"After breakfast, I started out walking to see the town. The innkeeper told me to go to the London Coffee House. Men met there to conduct business. I passed a bakery on the way and bought a puffy roll for a penny."

Ollie, Thomas's beagle, kept nudging Thomas for another scrap from the table. Even though Thomas was listening to Papa's every word, the four-year-old made sure his mama didn't see him give Ollie anything.

"I met some other Scots-Irish men at the London Coffee House that morning. They were going to move westward into Pennsylvania. I was able to find work with them.

"The next time I was at the London Coffee House, I met your Grandpa Barry. He was on a business trip to Philadelphia. Grandpa was traveling back to his home here in Anson the next day. We talked a long time. Your grandpa invited me to follow him to Carolina. I left with him and ten other Scots-Irish families early the next morning.

"The Great Philadelphia Wagon Road was heavily traveled. Traders went down it with their packhorses loaded sometimes with six hundred pounds of goods. Livestock was on its way to market. Once in a while we met herds of sheep, cattle, and pigs all in the same day. There were also other families on their way to settle new farms and start new lives. It was a very busy road."

Elizabeth, the baby, started fussing in her cradle. Mama picked her up to rock her.

The other children didn't seem to hear their baby sister and continued listening to their father.

"One day we saw Indian tracks on the road. Even though the Indian wars were over, it made us all a little nervous. That same night an Indian trader stopped by our camp. We invited him to eat supper with us. We all tried to be good neighbors to everyone we met. The trader told us the Iroquois called the wagon road the Ancient Warrior's Trail."

"Papa, did you know that is why I call myself Mighty Warrior when I am pretending to be an Indian?" interrupted Thomas. "Ollie and I pretend we are in the forest tracking deer."

"Yes, and you scared me this very day, Thomas!" exclaimed Alice. "You jumped out from behind those bushes and hollered at me! I dropped my basket of blackberries all over the ground. We didn't have a fruit pie tonight because of you!"

"I sure didn't mean to make you spill the blackberries, Alice. I just wanted to scare you. I am sorry," apologized Thomas.

"Thomas, you must have learned a valuable lesson this afternoon about being careful when you scare someone. Is that right?"

"Yes, sir, Papa. I will surely look to see if Alice is carrying a berry basket next time."

Before he laughed aloud at Thomas' apology, Charles quickly began again. "We traveled through the beautiful Shenandoah Valley all the way through Virginia into North Carolina. Grandpa Barry told me that the Philadelphia Road covered almost eight hundred miles. Nothing was easy about the journey, but it was never boring.

"I was reading a copy of Poor Richard's Almanac by the fire one night. Your grandpa was already asleep. I read one of those wise sayings that Ben Franklin was always adding to his almanac. 'A true friend is the best possession,' he wrote. You know, children, those months I traveled the Great Philadelphia Road with your grandpa and the rest of our group that has settled here in Anson County, I met some mighty fine friends. These have been really good years. That Master Franklin must have some good friends, too."

"Charles, is this a good time to tell the children what you have decided?" asked Mary. She put down the baby as she spoke.

"Yes, my darling, I think it is," Charles answered.

"I would like to call a Moore family meeting. There is something important I want to tell all of you."

Kate and Alice put down their handwork. The third daughter, Rosa, was playing with a sock doll, pretending it was a baby. The younger daughters, Mary, Violet, and Rachel, were getting sleepy but straightened up at their papa's words. They all looked at him expectantly. He didn't call many family meetings. Thomas's feet were still for once.

"What good memories I have of my time here in North Carolina. Your Grandpa Barry brought me here, and then I met your mama. We built our first home together. Anson County has been good to us."

Mary and Charles smiled at each other. "All of you were born here. This is the only home you know, but our family has an opportunity to be adventurers together.

"We are going to move to South Carolina, children. In fact, we are not the only families leaving Anson County. More settlers are moving here every day. I applied for and received a land grant from King George III for five hundred and fifty acres. Many of our friends are going with us. I have heard it is beautiful land, and your mama and I know we will be happy there. We are going to start packing tomorrow and will leave in two weeks.

"Now, it's your turn. Tell me what you think of my news?"

Immediately the room filled with questions from the seven children. Their manners were forgotten as all spoke at once. Charles and Mary answered them, but it took a while. It was long after the children's bedtime when the Moore family finally blew out the candles and Charles banked the fire in the fireplace.

Before he shut his eyes that night, Thomas sleepily said to Ollie, "We are going to the Tyger River, Ollie. Won't we have fun!"

# 3

# TRAVELING TO
# THE UPCOUNTRY

Thomas woke up that morning and jumped out of bed. He started repeating, "We are going to the Upcountry! We are going to the Upcountry!"

He pulled up his breeches and put on his vest. He had worn his shirt to bed. There was no reason for shoes because it was so warm.

The whole Moore family was excited about going to their new home in the Upcountry of South Carolina.

Margaret Catherine was the oldest of the Moore children. Everyone called her Kate. She was eleven and dressed quickly. She was going to help Mama make breakfast. The oatmeal was already cooking in the iron pot in the fireplace. Ten-year-old Alice worked a brush through Rosa's tangled hair. Rachel and Violet could put on their own dresses now, but Mary still helped them. Baby Elizabeth was still in her cradle. She certainly was no trouble to get ready. She would travel mostly in her cradle. Papa already had a place in the wagon for her.

Finally they all sat down for breakfast. It was

only 5:00 a.m. They heard the crowing of the roosters outside. Then Papa bowed his head. Everyone was quiet, even the roosters. "Thank you, Lord, for this day. Thank you for the food you have given us. Thank you for this home, and thank you for our new home. Keep us all safe, Father, as we travel. We depend on you to look after us. In Jesus' name, we pray, Amen."

Suddenly the children all talked at once. They talked to each other and asked questions of their parents.

"Are the other families ready to go?" asked Kate.

"Yes," replied Mama. "They have been packing just like we have."

Thomas patted Ollie under the table. "Do you think Ollie can walk all the way to the Upcountry, Papa? Can he ride in the wagon if he gets tired?"

Papa took his time answering Thomas. In fact, he sipped some more tea before he answered his son.

"Thomas, you have asked that question every day for the past two weeks. The answer is still yes! We are all going to walk on the road sometimes, and we will ride in the wagon sometimes. And that includes Ollie!"

Seven-year-old Mary asked the question that was on everyone's mind.

"How long will it take us to get to our new home, Papa?"

"We are not sure about that, Mary. I talked to a trader who said a loaded wagon can not go far in one day, but it shouldn't take too long."

"Is our wagon loaded with plenty of food?" Thomas wanted to know.

Both Mama and Papa laughed. Thomas was always hungry. He often said, "I'm starving to death!"

No one was surprised at his question. He had trouble sitting still. He liked to run or play with Ollie all the time. He had a lot of energy. He was going to enjoy every day of their journey.

The day before, Mama had baked some extra corn dodgers for the trip. She didn't want Thomas to get too hungry on the first day of their journey.

Kate was quiet during breakfast. She helped her younger sisters to finish quickly. But inside she was nearly bursting with excitement. Papa had finally bought Kate her first pony. She had practiced riding him every day for weeks. His name was George. Kate was going to ride him to the Upcountry of South Carolina. Papa had promised. She even had a new sidesaddle. All the ladies rode sidesaddle. Kate couldn't wait to leave.

The sun was just peaking over the mountains as the wagons lined up. Eleven other families were traveling with the Moores, and each was looking forward to a new life in South Carolina. One of the families was the Barry brothers— Andrew, Richard, and John Barry—who shared a Conestoga wagon.

Seventeen-year-old Andrew Barry chose to ride

Conestoga Wagon

his horse that day. He was in front of the brothers' wagon and shouted, "Let's go to the Upcountry!"

Each wagon fell in line. Some rode on horseback, like Kate and Andrew. Many children walked. Some men herded the sheep and cattle they were taking with them. It was quite a caravan. Most smiled and talked in excited voices. There were tears, too.

They were all leaving family, and they knew they might never return to Anson County.

The group followed the Great Philadelphia Road. There was something new to see around every bend in the road.

They heard wolves howling almost every night. Their howling always scared the children and made the livestock skittish. It was hard for the adults to sleep, too. The men took turns staying up to guard the camp. Each man would stand a four-hour watch around the camp. Then another man would take his place for his four hours of duty. Their rifles were always in their hands, and they made sure their powder horns were full and dry.

The first week it rained four days in a row. The children were bored with riding in the wagon. There wasn't enough room to get comfortable. Everyone was cranky and tired of trying to best each other by saying tongue twisters. No one wanted to hear "She sheared six shabby sick sheep" ever again. They were even tired of the cold food. It was too wet to build a cooking fire.

Mama decided to teach them a new song. Rachel and Violet sat in Mama's lap. Kate held Elizabeth to let her out of the cradle for a while. Alice helped Thomas clap his hands on rhythm. Rosa and Mary easily learned the words as Mama sang.

*Go tell Aunt Rhody,*
*Go tell Aunt Rhody,*
*Go tell Aunt Rhody,*
*The old gray goose is dead.*

*The one that she's been savin',*
*The one that she's been savin',*
*The one that she's been savin',*
*To make a feather bed.*

*She died in the millpond.*
*She died in the millpond.*

*She died in the millpond.*
*From standin' on her head.*

*The goslins are crying.*
*The goslins are crying.*
*The goslins are crying.*
*Because their mammy's dead.*

*The gander is weeping.*
*The gander is weeping.*
*The gander is weeping.*
*Because his wife is dead.*

Soon the sound of the rain brought the sound of happy voices.

The next week they stopped for two days to repair some of the wagons. Althought the Conestoga wagons were made well, the hidden rocks in the road sometimes did a lot of damage. Mama unpacked her lye soap. The Moore girls helped Mama wash clothes in a nearby creek while they waited. They pounded the clothes on rocks and then rinsed them in the water.

Eventually everyone ended up bathing or swimming in the creek. Ollie tried to help, so he had a bath, too. No one was safe that day from Mama's lye soap.

Each day at least one of the children asked, "Are we there yet?"

The adventure Papa promised was getting tiresome. There were new struggles every day. All the children were weary of walking or bouncing in the wagons. Sometimes Kate let one of them ride with her on George. Finally even that was no longer a treat.

Nothing was easy about the journey. Each day the men hunted for food to feed their families for supper. The parents constantly reminded the children to watch for snakes or poison ivy around the trail. Every night they went to sleep on the hard ground. Children became sick, and there was no doctor. Sometimes it was hard to find the right herbs to treat a fever. They stopped for several days because so many were puny. One day some robbers tried to steal from them.

But the families had a goal, and there was no turning back. Their new homes were ahead of them now in the Upcountry of South Carolina, not behind them in Anson County, North Carolina.

One morning Kate asked Papa wearily, "Are we there yet?"

Papa smiled and then laughed. "We will be there by noon, Kate!"

The Moore children clapped and shouted. Thomas threw his tricorn hat in the air. Papa helped Kate saddle George. The girls and Thomas started dancing down the road with Ollie right it the middle of them.

# 4

# LIFE ON
# THE TYGER RIVER

The dirt road ended, and there was the river.

Everyone could see it in the distance. The men urged their horses to move faster. Mothers shouted, "Be careful," to their children. All the children raced ahead of their parents.

Kate wanted to be the first one in the river. She talked to her pony, George. "Come on, George. I know you are thirsty. I know you can run really fast. Let's go get some water!"

George perked up his ears and galloped past everyone, including Thomas and Ollie. Thomas frowned and hollered for Kate to wait for him. Once again Kate leaned over and whispered more encouraging words to George. He picked up speed again. In a few minutes Kate laughed out loud as George galloped into the river. Immediately, they were both drenched. Kate did not mind the cold water. She was excited to win the race.

Kate was glad that George was starting to listen to her when she talked to him. He seemed to understand exactly what she said.

Andrew Barry was riding beside Papa. He

Panther

asked, "Are you sure this is the Tyger River?"

"That it is," said Papa. "The French trapper said that the Tyger River was our next landmark. We need to remind everyone, especially the children, about those tigers he said were about. I have only read about tigers living in India or Africa, but he sure did warn us to be careful. Perhaps they are like the panthers we saw in North Carolina near Salisbury."

All thirteen Conestoga wagons soon made it to the river. They saw minnows feeding behind the rocks and shiny bass jumping out of the water. Some of the boys found a turtle sunning itself on a rock. Along the water's edge, they saw deer tracks and even some bear tracks. Mama was glad to see the flock of ducks flying overhead. Their feathers would make good ticking for mattresses.

Thomas laughed when he heard the distant gobble-gobble of some wild turkeys. Thomas spoke to the beagle, as he rubbed his own tummy, "Ollie, you will really enjoy one of those turkey legs."

Ollie showed his usual excitement by running in circles.

It was a wilderness, and it was their new home.

There was no time to stand and look at this natural beauty. They had to get their campsite ready for the night. Mama wanted to bake some cornbread in her Dutch oven for supper. She needed some kindling to start a fire and a spit made to cook on. Papa pulled his broad ax out of the wagon to start that job.

Thomas's job was to clear a place in the grass for the fire. The girls went to the river to find rocks for fire stones. Elizabeth needed her pudding cap put on so she could walk around. Kate was put in charge of Elizabeth.

As Kate followed Elizabeth around the river, she began to sing to her.

*The farmer's in the dell,*
*The farmer's in the dell,*
*Hi! Ho! The derry oh,*
*The farmer's in the dell.*

Soon many of the children were singing along

with Kate as they worked together with their parents.

The next morning all the families met together. The men decided on a plan. Each family was going to separate from the group to find its own land. Then everyone would take turns working together on a cabin-raising and land clearing for their neighbors. If everyone worked together, all would have shelter and fall crops in the ground before cold weather.

Their plan worked.

Building cabins and clearing fields took a long time. They also had to dig wells or else find a spring for fresh water. The families lived out of the Conestoga wagons or built lean-tos for protection from the weather.

The Moore family was happy to move out of the lean-to Papa built. That temporary shelter was too crowded for ten people. Their first house in South Carolina was a log cabin. They had to cut down eighty trees to build it. The fireplace was made out of rocks from the river. They used river mud for chinking the fireplace and logs. It was only one room, but Papa also designed a sleeping loft. The children raced each other up the ladder every night. Ollie learned to quickly get out of the way of the ladder when Mama said, "Time for bed, children."

The children heard stories of bears breaking into other cabins looking for food. But they were never afraid. Papa was strong. Every night he pulled the ladder up and closed the trapdoor. Then

Papa slept on top of the door with his musket by his side all night.

Besides shelter, the family needed food to survive in the wilderness. The closest city was Charles Town, and it was over two hundred miles away. Traveling down the old Cherokee Trail for supplies took time away from the farm. Mama was always glad to greet one of the Indian traders when they came by her house. The traders or wagoners brought salt, sugar, and other supplies on pack horses to sell or trade.

But the family still needed vegetables. It was hard work to cut down so many trees and clear the

First log house

brush before the ground was plowed. Because they had no equipment to remove the tree stumps, they planted around the stumps. The children planted seeds and kept the weeds pulled. They planted corn, cabbage, potatoes, and beans. The corn was very important, because both the family and the animals ate it. Mama made cornbread every day, especially those corn dodgers that Thomas liked.

Kate stayed right beside her mama all day long. She watched everything Mama did. Kate asked a lot of questions about quilting, cooking, making soap and candles, and churning butter. Mother and daughter talked constantly as they went from one chore to another. Kate was eager to learn, and Mama was a good teacher. Mama depended on Kate, because she was the oldest daughter. The younger children demanded a lot of attention, too. They constantly needed bandages and hugs when they fell or discipline when they were disobedient.

But it was not all work every day. Papa sometimes declared a family holiday. They invited the neighbors over for picnics and horse races. The Barry brothers came often from their farm next to the Moores' farm. The youngest children chose teams for a race. Hide-and-seek was a favorite, and Kate always found the best hiding places. Duck-duck-goose was Rachel and Violet's favorite game, and they enjoyed picking the grown-ups for the goose.

Mama and Papa loved to sing, and they taught their children many songs. Singing helped the work seem less like work.

Papa always kept at least one musket handy wherever he went. Papa and Mama already knew how to shoot a musket. So did Kate and Alice. One day Papa decided it was time to teach Rosa, Mary, Rachel, and Violet how to use a musket. They were not strong enough to load the musket themselves. He taught them about how much powder to put in the barrel and how to load the lead balls in the musket. Thomas was about to turn green with jealousy as he watched his sisters.

One afternoon Papa turned to Thomas, "Are you ready to try, Thomas?"

What a day that was for Thomas! With his papa's help, he loaded a musket for the first time. The girls did not practice every day, but Thomas did. He looked forward to going hunting with Papa. It was not long before that first hunting trip happened.

Finding fresh meat to eat was never a problem for the family, because it was plentiful. The men and boys hunted deer, buffalo, and raccoons. Thomas helped Papa make a hat out of the first raccoon he killed. He was proud of his coonskin hat, and he wore it every day. There was an abundance of squirrels, rabbits, and turkeys nearby. Turkeys sometimes weighed as much as fifty pounds, and their meat would last several days.

Papa made extra money by raising and selling livestock. He and Thomas made many trips to Hannah's Cow Pens to sell their extra cattle. Everyone in the Upcountry knew where those cow pens were. Men taking their cattle to market in Charles Town often stopped there to rest their herds. It was a good place to find out the latest news.

Indians were a danger to the families every day. These Scots-Irish settled in the Cherokee's hunting grounds. One day, their neighbor John Miller was ambushed and killed by Indians while walking across the road at the shoals of the Tyger River. After this incident, the men decided to build a fort for protection. They called it Nicholls Fort because it was close to Master Nicholls' grist mill. Whenever the alarm sounded, the families went to the fort for protection. Before long, other communities built small forts to protect themselves. There was safety in numbers.

After two years of living in their log cabin, the Moore family moved into their new home. Charles built the two-story farmhouse close to the log cabin.

The keeping room was the family's favorite room in the house. The trunks that Charles and Mary brought with them from Ireland had a special place. Their family Bible was important to all of them. They kept the Bible, along with other important papers, in the Bible box near the front door. In case of fire, the box could easily be carried to safety. There were blocks, dominoes, a goose and dice game, cards, and many books to read. The family gathered there every night to play games and to hold family devotions.

Charles and Mary never forgot the reasons

they left Ireland and came to America. The Catholics mocked the Presbyterians, and the laws would not allow the Scots-Irish to prosper. Their Presbyterian faith and independence from British laws were important to them. They were thankful to be in America.

Sunday was a special day, and they meant to honor the commandment to keep it holy. Their congregation called themselves the Tyger River Congregation. At first there was no church building. On many Sundays the families all met together in one of their private homes to hold a church service. When the weather was bad, they worshipped at home as a family. Papa would read the Bible and pray. Then they would sing psalms.

In 1765 the families built the first log meeting house in the upcountry. It was hard to decide where to build their church building. They all lived so far away from each other. There was much discussion before they approved a plan.

Everyone was excited the day they chose the land. A member of the congregation from the lower part of the settlement started walking north from his house. At the same time, a member from the upper part of the settlement started walking south. As the men walked, their families walked with them. Sometimes a family had to have a wagon for the younger children. Every time they walked past a new house, a new family joined the walk. It was like two parades. No one knew where they would meet. They finally met on John Caldwell's land grant.

They celebrated choosing the new place for their meeting house. The wives had packed food, and all the families put the food together for a dinner on the ground. That day was so much fun for everyone that a new tradition started. Every year the families celebrated the church's founding with a dinner gathering at the church. The name chosen was Nazareth Presbyterian Church.

# The Art of Housewifery

There were many daily routines in the Moore household. Each child had specific chores to learn and complete. New responsibilities came with a new birthday. Thomas followed his father and became skillful with the musket and the many farm chores. Each day Mary taught her seven daughters the art of housewifery. She wanted them to be good wives and mothers.

Like other Upcountry families, the Moores owned slaves to help them with the daily work. The men helped Charles in the fields, and Nancy helped Mama. Nancy was Mama's extra pair of hands. Nancy spun most of the flax into linen for their clothes. Her spinning wheel was in the kitchen. Often Mama depended on Nancy to watch Elizabeth and Thomas. The two youngest never minded being sent to the kitchen because they both knew that Nancy kept cookies there for them. While Nancy cooked or spun, they would race up and down the ladder to the loft. Nancy lived upstairs in the loft.

"Mercy," said Mama as she walked into the house. "It took us a long time to weed the herb and vegetable gardens this morning."

Mama hung her bonnet on the peg next to the back door. She never went outside without covering her head. All seven girls hung their bonnets up, too. Mama taught them that they needed to protect their skin from the sun and weather. The sun would give them freckles and wrinkle their skin. There was tansy in the herb garden to keep their faces white and smooth. At the first sign of freckles, Mama picked the leaves and soaked them in buttermilk for nine days. Then she put the leaves on the girls' faces. None of Mama's girls minded because the leaves had such a good smell.

"I am so glad that Papa built the cistern close to the gardens," said Rosa. "The rain-water is right there for us to use on the plants. We don't have to take our buckets to the river anymore. Water gets very heavy when I have to carry it too far."

"Shall we all have a drink of water ourselves before we start the washing? Kate, would you help your sisters, please?" Mama depended on Kate.

The kitchen building was in their original log cabin. Mama went over to check the pot of potatoes that was cooking over the fire. Nancy had watched to be sure the potatoes didn't burn while she was spinning. For seasoning in the potatoes, Mama added a little rosemary to the pot. There was cabbage already washed, chopped, and ready for Nancy to cook Any green vegetable that could be cooked and eaten was called salad. The ham was in the smokehouse ready to be brought in. Mama planned on making a fruit cobbler in between chores that afternoon.

Monday was always wash day. It was easier in the warm weather. In the summer it did not matter if the children got wet along with the clothes. Mama had checked the fire under the big iron pot before they went inside. It was full of clothes. The water had to be hot to get the clothes clean.

Kate picked up the gourd they used as a dipper. It was hanging beside the cedar bucket full of fresh water from their spring. One of Thomas's chores was to fill the bucket three times a day. He did not forget very often, because he was always thirsty.

With a smile on her face, Elizabeth jumped up and down. "Please, Kate, me first. Me first!" she exclaimed. With six older sisters, Elizabeth counted on them to take care of her first.

There was a sampler in Mama and Papa's room hanging beside the fireplace. Mama had stitched it when she was a girl. Pretty flowers were all around the border. The words were Mama's rules for running her household. Mama had learned them from her own mother.

Even Elizabeth could recite the words on the sampler.

*Wash on Monday.*
*Iron on Tuesday.*
*Mend on Wednesday.*
*Churn on Thursday.*
*Clean on Friday.*

*Bake on Saturday.*
*Rest on Sunday.*

The water in the iron pot was still hot when Mama and her daughters went back outside. Rachel and Violet rubbed the clothes with soap. Mama and Kate had made the soap from ashes they saved from the fireplace all winter. Kate scented some of the soap with lavender from the herb garden. The girls chose the lavender soap to use today, and everyone enjoyed the fragrant smell.

Rosa and Mary beat the clothes with small sticks to loosen the dirt. The sticks were smooth, so they did not tear the clothes. Several times Mama called them down for playing a tune with the sticks rather than helping to clean the clothes. Elizabeth entertained them all by blowing soap bubbles.

There were two wooden tubs nearby for rinsing the clothes. Kate and Alice were assigned that job. They washed quilts that day. The quilts were too heavy for one person when they were wet. It took Mama, Kate, and Alice to wring most of the water out of the quilts and then hang them on the line.

Ollie came back from his hunting trip to the river and promptly got in the way of the girls. He wanted to play. Elizabeth was put in charge of playing with Ollie. She blew soap bubbles at him and laughed when the bubbles burst on his nose.

Mama and her daughters worked well together. They talked and laughed a lot.

Tuesday was ironing day. The irons were

"Ollie"

placed close to the fireplace to get them hot. None of the girls liked to iron. Mama was very particular about the way it should be done. Even Papa's handkerchiefs were ironed. Sometimes the girls had to iron those handkerchiefs over and over until Mama finally said, "You did a good job. I am proud of you." Mama always added a hug and kiss to her words.

Alice told Mama that she had a terrible headache. Mama went straight to the herb garden to pick some mint to make tea. All women knew how to doctor with herbs. Mama made enough tea for all of the girls to enjoy a cup before they went back to ironing. She knew that sometimes an ounce of prevention was worth a pound of cure.

Wednesday was mending day. Sometimes they sat on the porch with their sewing. In the wintertime, they gathered around the fireplace. They needed light from the fire to see well. There were only four, small windows in the keeping room. The younger girls would work on splits in their pinafores or loose threads in their mob caps.

All women wore mob caps. It was a plain cap that was gathered with a frill. They were made of cotton. The caps protected their hair. No girl or lady would be seen in public without her head covered.

Kate, Alice, and Rosa would mend socks, stockings, or quilts. The girls were very particular about mending the stockings. They used some of the stockings to pull over the goose's head to blind him as they picked his feathers. If there was the smallest hole in the stocking, the angry goose would stick his beak out of the hole and bite whoever was pulling out his feathers. Rosa was the last one bitten by a goose. It was just not a fun chore.

The family needed those goose feathers, even though they came with a price. They stuffed the soft feathers of the geese in their quilts and pillows. Each year the girls pulled and collected new feathers to replace the old ones.

Mama worked on their dresses with the smallest stitches any of the girls had seen. She would often restitch the seams in Thomas's breeches or shirts. He was always tearing his clothes but never seemed to know how it happened. No matter how hard Mama and the girls worked on Wednesday, there was always another tall stack of mending waiting the next Wednesday.

Thursday was churning day. Mama's sampler said it was. None of the children understood that. Papa and Thomas milked the cows every day. That meant every day was churning day. The milk would go bad if they didn't take care of it. No one could drink all the milk from their herd in one day. Each day a cow produced about five gallons of milk. Thomas did not like to get out of bed early in the morning. Papa told him that there was no way he could milk all the cows without Thomas's help. Papa's compliment helped some. Ollie was ready to go to the barn every morning. He ran and turned in circles all the way. Ollie knew he would get a squirt of warm milk for his breakfast. The cows always greeted the three with much mooing.

The whole family drank milk for breakfast. Mama put some of the leftover milk in a five-gallon, stoneware jar called a crock. The crock was the churn. It had a wooden lid with a hole in the middle. She left the milk in the churn over night. By morning, the milk was sour and didn't smell sweet anymore. The milk had to turn sour or clabber before it could be churned into butter. Mama and her daughters took turns pushing the wooden paddle called a dasher up and down in the churn until the butter rose to the top. When the butter rose to the top of the crock, Mama used her butter pat to lift it out.

One day when no one was around, Thomas decided he would help his mama by churning. He forgot to put the lid on the churn. The milk went all over Mama's clean floor when Thomas pushed the dasher up and down. Mama helped him remember not to forget to put the lid on again!

It usually took thirty to forty minutes of churning for the milk to turn to butter. Sometimes Mama and Kate would put the butter into butter molds. The butter would have a design on it from the mold. Kate's favorite mold had a three-leaf clover cut in it. Papa cut out that design. He said it reminded him of the clover in Ireland. They kept the extra butter in the spring house. It was cool there. The butter melted quickly on hot cornbread or in oatmeal.

Friday was cleaning day The children went barefoot in the warm weather. Sometimes they wore moccasins like the Indians did. They saved their shoes for church on Sunday. That meant they tracked in a lot of dirt. Kate would sweep the floors in the morning, but before noon they were dirty again.

Even the dustless shelves had to be cleaned. The soot from the fireplaces usually fell off the shelves, but there was always some dust. Elizabeth said Mama had eagle eyes.

Elizabeth made sure there was no dust left anywhere in the house. She used a feather duster made from the goose feathers to dust the furniture. Mama insisted that she even dust the warming pans.

Papa was a good carpenter, and he made a lot of their furniture. Mama was proud of everything that Papa did and very particular about the cleaning of that furniture. When Elizabeth finished dusting, Mama checked to see if there was any dust left behind. Mama would take a white cloth and rub it over the furniture. If there was any dust on the cloth, Elizabeth did not pass white glove inspection. Then Elizabeth started dusting again.

The younger girls usually took the rag rugs out to clean them. They would beat them with sticks on the porch. They had to sweep under the beds. Mama was not happy when she found dust bunnies. Every week they found some of Thomas's

marbles under the furniture.

Mama taught Kate how to make stew. It cooked all day over the fire in the fireplace. Cleaning day was a good day for stew. After killing the chicken, they would scald it. That made it easier to pluck out the feathers. Papa did not like feathers in the stew. Mama always made a large pot of stew. She would add onions, carrots, peas, and potatoes to the chicken. Sage was a good herb for flavor. Sometimes she just added new vegetables to the pot, and the family ate it again the next day.

Mama did not believe in wasting anything. She taught the girls a rhyme that she had learned from her mama. "Peas porridge hot. Peas porridge cold. Peas porridge in the pot nine days old. Some like it hot. Some like it cold. Some like it in the pot nine days old."

All the girls enjoyed the baking that went on every Saturday. The baking started on Friday night. Mama and Kate would mix the dough and then knead it. The younger girls were learning to push the dough with their palms and pull it back to them. When the dough was kneaded, they covered it and left it overnight. It was ready to bake the next morning in their small brick oven in the kitchen.

Thomas did not mind going to milk the cows on Saturday. He liked Saturday because Mama made Johnny cakes for breakfast. Mama needed extra milk for those cakes. After she measured the cornmeal with her hands, she was ready for the milk. Sometimes Thomas was so excited he would run back to the house from the barn with the milk for his mama. Ollie always tried to catch any drops that fell from the bucket.

After Mama mixed the cakes, she fried the corn meal cakes in butter in the skillet. The family usually ate them hot with butter and preserves or molasses. Elizabeth liked hers with sugar. Kate would cut sugar off the large cone of sugar with the sugar cutter and bring it to the table. Elizabeth always thanked her big sister with wide smiles.

Mama taught her daughters how to tell the difference between a hot and a warm fire. The heat from the oven would burn the bread or pies if it was too hot. Mama timed her baking by watching a candle burn down. The cornbread was ready to take out of the oven when a candle burned all the way down. Kate could already tell by watching the wick on the candle burn when a pie was ready to come out of the oven. When the candle burned halfway down the wick, it was time. The girls learned at an early age how important it was to keep the fire going. Without the fire, cooking was impossible. The home fire had to be kept burning. It took all day to plan and cook the meals for the family.

Mama was very patient as she taught her daughters the art of housewifery. She wanted them to be able to take care of their own husbands and children one day. Mama also taught them good manners. Each daughter learned how to curtsy, pour tea, and dress properly. They learned the importance of hospitality and how to make guests feel welcome in the home. Mama modeled what she taught her daughters. She loved them dearly and never let a day go by without telling them she was proud of them.

Elizabeth often mimicked Mama by spreading her arms wide and saying, "You are the sweetest girl in the whole wide world."

# 6

# ANDREW BARRY

It was the spring of 1767. Kate was going to marry Andrew Barry. She was fifteen, and Andrew was twenty-one.

Kate remembered the first time she had really noticed Andrew. It was the day they left Anson County, North Carolina, to travel to the Upcountry. The three Barry brothers were good friends of the Moore family. They all went to the same church.

Andrew, Richard, and John Barry had stood by their lead wagon that cold morning. They all laughed and talked at the same time. Andrew kept checking the harnesses on the oxen. As he walked around the Conestoga wagon, he intently pushed on every board. He even kicked the wheels on the wagon.

As Andrew patted his horse and talked to him, his brothers teased him, "Andrew, you have been checking and rechecking all our supplies for days now. You sure take after Papa with being sure everything is in order. Do you even remember how that used to drive you crazy when he would come and check behind you like that?"

Kate noticed the way he smiled at his brothers and kept on checking. She liked his smile and the way he took their teasing. There was a twinkle in his blue eyes.

Kate saw his kindness to Ollie on the trail one day. Ollie liked to chase anything that moved. That day he chased a squirrel. The squirrel hid under the roots of a large tree. Ollie tried to use his front paws to dig where the squirrel was. One of Ollie's paws got stuck, and he started howling. Thomas tried to get Ollie's paw loose, but he could not do it. Andrew came to help, but Ollie snapped and growled him. Andrew paid Ollie no mind and kept easing his paw out. Finally the paw slipped loose. Andrew's hands were bleeding, but Ollie was free. Thomas and Ollie both jumped up in Andrew's arms to thank him.

Kate liked the way Andrew wouldn't stop until Ollie was loose. He was a determined and kind man. He took time with children and animals.

Kate saw how quickly Andrew reacted the day the Nicholls boy fell off the roof of his house. A tall oak tree had fallen on the house during a storm. The men in the community were helping Master Nicholls put on a new roof. The women were involved in a quilting bee while they watched the children.

Andrew reached the boy first, and Kate heard him say a quick prayer. When Master Nicholls reached his son, Andrew quickly let him know his son was fine. Kate was not surprised that Andrew was chosen as one of the first elders in Nazareth

Presbyterian Church.

Andrew had been nineteen years old when his family settled on the Tyger River. The three Barry brothers were the Moores' closest neighbors. It had not taken them long to build their log cabin or start clearing their land. They were not lazy, and they were all strong. Thomas wanted to be as tall and strong as Andrew. Thomas said Andrew was six feet two inches tall.

All three brothers had received a good education and were interested in politics.

They also had definite ideas about the difference between right and wrong. Papa said the Barry men were expert riflemen and did not waste any shot. As more people moved into the Upcountry, there was more lawlessness. Cattle rustlers and horse thieves were a problem.

The nearest law officers were in Charles Town. For protection from law breakers, the men from Anson County organized a militia. The Barry brothers were all members. Andrew was the captain. He was always ready to protect his neighbors and friends. Kate knew Andrew was dependable and trustworthy.

On the day Papa talked to Kate about marrying Andrew, Papa had a serious look on his face. Andrew had written a letter asking Papa's permission to court her. After Papa read her the letter, he gave the letter to Kate.

*Dear Sir:*
*In the absence of my father, I am writing you*

*of my intentions to your daughter, Kate.*

*I would be glad of your consent in addressing and pursuing marriage with Kate. I own one hundred acres of the best farmland and can support a wife and family. My affairs are in good order, and there are no debts. I promise that I will, to the best of my ability, love and honor Kate for the rest of my life. It would be both my privilege and commitment to take care of her in the manner to which she is accustomed.*

*Sincerely,*
*Andrew Barry*

After Kate read the letter for herself, she questioned Papa with her eyes.

With a smile now on his face, Papa said, "He is a good man, Kate. Andrew has good character and common sense. I am ready to give him permission to marry you. What do you think about Andrew as a husband, my dear daughter? If that is agreeable with you, I am ready to write him back with an answer and discuss an agreement."

As she hugged her father, Kate replied, "Oh, yes, Papa, that is quite agreeable to me." Papa wrote Andrew back.

*Dear Sir:*

*I received your letter asking for the hand of my daughter in marriage. You are a man of good character. You have applied for my leave to make addresses to Kate. I freely give my permission. As your wife, she will bring to this marriage one hundred acres of land, a herd of cattle, and other personal properties. I look forward to discussing this further with you at your earliest convenience.*

*Sincerely,*
*Charles Moore*


The courtship of Kate and Andrew began. Andrew frequently visited Kate at her home. Mama often asked him to share meals with them. One day Elizabeth innocently asked, "Andrew, why don't you just move in with us? You are here all the time."

The family laughed. The couple had been very careful of propriety. Kate and Andrew were never alone. Their walks were chaperoned. Even when they sat and talked on the front porch, one or more of the sisters was always nearby.

Mama and Kate talked about little else but "the wedding."

Kate's sisters were so excited. The wedding was going to be at their home. There would be a party afterwards to celebrate the marriage. A wedding dress had to be made. Lace had to be picked out. Fabric would be ordered from Charles Town. Mama had read the advertisement of the milliner, Katherine Lind, in the *South Carolina Gazette*. Her list of thread, collars, lace, ribbons, and gloves was lengthy. Mama decided to order many items from Mrs. Lind's shop on Tradd Street in Charles Town.

Andrew Barry

Mama's list grew each day. Kate was going to use part of Papa's handkerchief that he brought from Ireland in her veil. More linens were needed to fill Kate's hope chest. Nancy had spun the flax into thread for the linen material for Kate's sheets and pillowcases. Kate still had more tatting to finish on the pillowcases. There was a menu to be planned to feed the guests. Mama hoped there was enough time.

Kate believed this was the most important step of her life. She was ready to become the beloved wife of Andrew Barry.

# 7

# Rocky Springs Academy

It was Sunday, and the Moore family was having a quiet afternoon.

Thomas was unhappy. Mama had sent all of her communion wafers to Mrs. Nicholls the day before. Papa had learned at the grist mill from Mr. Nicholls that his wife was sick and told Mama. Thomas dearly loved those flat cookies. He wished Mama had saved some for him.

Thomas was also tired. He and Papa had repaired the split rail fences on Saturday. His muscles were so sore. Thomas really wanted to be running outside with Ollie, but it was raining. Instead Thomas played inside with his marbles.

His older sisters worked on their samplers. Elizabeth was content playing with her church dolls. She pretended she was their mama. Mama was working on a quilt square. She never sat down without some kind of stitchery in her hands. Papa was reading his new copy of the *South Carolina Gazette*.

Suddenly Thomas stopped playing. He could not believe his ears. His mouth dropped open. He just knew his Papa was not serious. But Thomas could tell by Papa's tone of voice that he was very serious.

"Mary, I want to start a school. I have been thinking about it for weeks now. I want to build a schoolhouse on our land. All the families can pitch in to hire a teacher. He can take turns living with all the different families.

"I have a good library of books to share, and the Barry brothers brought books with them. We have *Aesop's Fables*. All our children have enjoyed hearing those fables.

"Do you remember how Kate would get them all to act out one of those tales?"

Elizabeth was listening to her papa as she played. She smiled, remembering the time she was the turtle. Thomas was the fox. Her sisters helped her beat Thomas in a race around the house. It was the first time she beat Thomas in a race.

"There is no reason not to share this knowledge with the other children that live close by." Papa stood up and walked around as he talked. The family could tell he was very excited.

"Every family has its own Bibles, hornbooks, and copies of *The New England Primer*. None of us really have the time to take from making a living to teach the children. I believe that all the children would learn better together in a classroom. What do you think, Mary?"

"Oh, Charles," said Mary. "That is a splendid idea. Can you talk to the other families next Sunday after church? We have the books our children have enjoyed hearing you read before they went to bed at night. You also have some that the boys would particularly enjoy. Where are your copies of *Robinson Crusoe*, *Gulliver's Travels*, and *Tales of King Arthur*?"

Thomas wanted to be a soldier. He knew he did not have to go to school for that. He liked nothing better than tracking raccoons and deer in the forest. He practiced his riflery by shooting at stumps every day. Latin and calculus would not help him to be a good soldier. Ten-year-old Thomas knew better than to say anything to his Papa. He did not want to hear that old saying, "Children are to be seen, not heard." He called Ollie inside. Thomas wanted to play with Ollie, not read more books. They quickly went up the stairs.

Rocky Springs Academy opened within three months. The year was 1770. The school was only two miles from the Moores' house. It had one room with four windows. There was a large fireplace for heat and light. The children sat in desks or on benches. Charles Moore was the first schoolmaster. He called the students his scholars. At age ten Thomas did not want to be a scholar. He wanted to be a soldier.

The students wrote with quill pens. Those quills were feathers pulled from the geese. Thomas liked to use his knife to sharpen the feathers for a pen. He liked to use his jackknife to whittle on wood, also. They made ink from walnut hulls, vinegar, and salt. The ink was kept in an ink well on each desk.

Master Moore kept fine sand from the Tyger River in the classroom. The students used it to sprinkle on the paper to help the ink dry faster or to soak up any mistakes. Master Moore called it pounce.

Each scholar had his or her own hornbook. Paper was very expensive. Using the hornbooks was a way to teach reading without using a lot of paper. On one side of the hornbook were the letters of the alphabet and numbers. Both small and capital letters were printed on the hornbooks. On the other side was a copy of the Lord's Prayer.

Most of the children could already recite the Lord's Prayer. It was easier to learn how to read from something familiar.

The hornbooks were shaped like small, wooden paddles, and the paper was attached to the board. To protect the paper and make it last longer, it was covered with a thin piece of cow's horn. Some of the hornbooks had a string through a hole in the handle. The young scholar would sometimes hold it around his neck or waist by the string.

One day Elizabeth raised her hand and said, "Papa, I remember when Mama made us a hornbook out of gingerbread. Every time we learned a letter, we got to eat that letter. I would like another gingerbread hornbook rather than this one, please. I believe I could learn to read much faster with the gingerbread letters."

Master Moore had to swallow his laughter before he answered Elizabeth. "We will talk about it later, Elizabeth."

There were several copies of *The New England Primer* in the classroom. These books were short and very small. They usually were only three inches by four inches long. Each page would have five letters on it with a picture that began with that letter. There would also be a rhyme about the letter. Thomas's favorite letter was "D." The rhyme for "D" was "The Dog will bite a Thief at Night." He told Ollie this quite often.

Master Moore liked to teach by using rhyme. One day he taught them a way to learn how many days there were in each month.

*Thirty days hath September,*
*April, June, and November.*
*All the rest have thirty-one.*
*Excepting February alone,*
*And it has twenty-eight days time,*
*But in leap years, February has twenty-nine.*

Thomas missed Elizabeth when she started staying at home with Mama. Girls only went to school until they learned the alphabet, spelling, writing, and simple math. Learning to read was important for reading the Bible. Math was important to be able to keep up with a home and household expenses. Now Mama was going to teach Elizabeth the art of housewifery just like she taught Kate, Alice, Rosa, Mary, Rachel and Violet.

There was a dunce cap on top of the dunce stool in the corner of the classroom. None of the students wanted to sit there. If a young scholar was lazy doing his work, Master Moore would send him to sit on the dunce stool and wear the dunce cap.

Thomas often spoke when he should have been listening. Then the cone-shaped cap would be on his head for a time. Master Moore believed that a short time on the dunce stool was a good reminder for his scholars He did not believe that a long time was necessary.

The students brought their lunches to school. It was too far for them to go home in the middle of the day. In the winter they would eat inside, and outside in the summer.

The schoolmaster believed that there was much knowledge to be learned outside. He encouraged them to play competitive games and to try their best. There was always a rope handy for a game of tug-of-war. They had foot races and arm wrestled. In the spring they made kites out of cloth and took them outside to see who would win with the highest-flying kite. Climbing trees and walking logs taught them agility. Alertness and speed were important to survive in this wilderness. The scholars learned how to tell direction from the moss on trees and when cold weather was approaching by a flock of geese flying south.

Master Moore expected them to keep their eyes open and their minds ready to learn at all times. Each day he repeated Poor Richard's words, "Do not squander Time, for that's what Life is made of."

These scholars at Rocky Springs Academy

learned their lessons by repeating them over and over. Some days were more boring than others. Greek and Latin were harder for Thomas to learn than calculus. But learn he did. He always won the contest by creating images from the seven shapes of the tangram puzzles. Animals were his favorite to put together. He was excited the day that he used those five triangles, one square, and one parallelogram of his tangrams to understand geometry.

The season of the year and the work to be done on each farm determined when most of the boys attended school. Their fathers depended on their sons to work beside them to keep the farms running smoothly. Rocky Springs Academy was the first community school in the Upcountry. Another of Papa's dreams was realized when he saw one after another of his neighbors' sons walk through the doors of that one-room schoolhouse.

# Unrest in
# the Upcountry

It was a beautiful spring day in May of 1777, and Charles and Mary Moore were expecting company.

"I see the horses and wagons," shouted Andrew.

Charlie shouted, "Mama, I see my friends!"

They jumped down from the mounting block and ran down the road.

Andrew was six, and Charlie was three. These two boys were the last of Mama and Papa's children. They were always together.

All the families of Nazareth Presbyterian Church were coming to the Moores' house today. Last year the families had celebrated the defeat of the British in Charles Town. That was when Sir Henry Clinton left the harbor without taking the port city.

Today they celebrated the signing of the Treaty of Dewitt's Corner. The settlers had fought for a year, and over two thousand Cherokee were killed because of the fierce fighting of the Upcountry militia. The Cherokee had finally asked for peace and had given up much of their land to South Carolina and Georgia.

The Cherokee had been a major threat to every home in the Upcountry. British agents incited the Indians to fight hard against the colonists to gain back their hunting grounds. The British used the Indians to help put down the colonists' rebellion against their own English government.

Scots-Irish families like the Moores and Barrys were determined to protect their homes and their children. Their militia units did more than just patrol the land against outlaws or Indian raids. They also elected officers, had regular meetings, and went on the offense against the Indians. Each man knew he could trust the men in his unit with his life.

There were other colonists who could not be trusted. Many stories were told about how some of those loyal to King George III, the king of England, had dressed up as Indians and attacked settlers along with the Cherokee. Homes were looted and burned, and the Indians took captives. The Scots-Irish in this Tyger River community were on constant alert. Children were kept close to the houses. Everyone carried a rifle to the fields. No one slept well at night. But one enemy was defeated now, and everyone was ready to celebrate the victory.

Reverend Joseph Alexander, the pastor of Nazareth Presbyterian Church, would come to lead them in a prayer of thanksgiving. There would be plenty of food. Nancy helped Mama

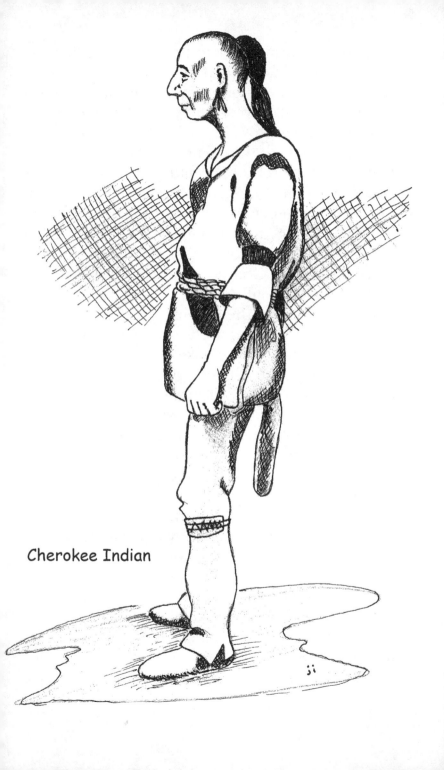

Cherokee Indian

prepare the extra tables to hold the food that the guests were bringing. Papa had promised a horse race to his two youngest boys. The slave men on the Moores' farm were ready to take care of the visitors' horses.

Kate and Andrew had arrived before breakfast that morning. Ten years had passed since their wedding. Their three children were still asleep in the wagon. Young Andrew and Charlie lost no time in waking their nephews and niece. Kate fussed at them both, but she smiled while she did.

Andrew and Charlie climbed the steps and went into the keeping room. There were always family members in the keeping room. It was their sitting room. "Mama, are we old enough to play tug-of-war yet?" Charlie asked.

"Oh, boys, you know that only grownups play that game. You will have fun playing leap-frog and Scotch-hopper with your friends. There will probably be a game of hide-and-seek this afternoon. You will probably win. Do you remember when Kate showed you all her hiding places?" Mama gave both boys a quick hug.

Mama continued, "Andrew, I need you to help Charlie take his wooden hobby horse to the porch, please. There will be some younger children here that will enjoy it today. I know you will want to share it."

Kate was filling another jar with molasses to put on the table. It would catch any flies or bugs that would be after the food on the table. The flies particularly liked the sugar in the molasses. Rather than landing on the food, the insects would go for the sugar and get stuck. Most of the women agreed that molasses was better than a fly swatter.

She was listening to Mama as Mama talked to her brothers. Kate was still surprised with everything that Mama remembered. It was no wonder that all the families in the community enjoyed coming to visit the Moore home.

Both Papa and Mama made everyone feel welcome. They taught their children that hospitality was important. Travelers on the road from Charles Town knew they could always find a hot meal and shelter at the Moore home. Kate and Andrew were beginning to earn that same reputation for being good neighbors.

The women started bringing their food to the kitchen. Soon there was ham, deer, and turkey a'plenty on the table. Many brought stews in their Dutch ovens. Just about every woman brought her own special recipe of corn pudding, spoonbread, corn dodgers, cornbread, and popped corn. There were fruit cobblers, cakes, and dozens of communion cakes. Kate put her jars of apple butter close to the biscuits and cornbread.

There was a smile on each woman's face. Laughter was heard from the windows. Only a few weeks ago fear had controlled them.

The men were standing together under the tree outside the house. Their rifles were close by. Rather than holding their rifles, many smoked their clay pipes. These men were in the same militia unit. They talked quietly about what they had seen in their fights to keep the Cherokee from taking their land back.

Master Nicholls asked, "Did you know that my neighbor, Master Ferguson, told me I was too stubborn in my ways? He is not from Ireland. Master Ferguson is from England. He said the British superintendent of Indian affairs had encouraged the Cherokee to attack us."

The men knew they had mostly been left alone by the Charles Town officials and England because they were so far away in the Upcountry. These Scots-Irish families both enjoyed and treasured their independence They were accustomed to taking care of themselves and each other. Each militia unit was made up of friends. They trusted each other. In their homes and meeting houses, they talked freely about their concerns.

"In one of those skirmishes the other week at the mill, one of those men loyal to the King took my sword. It has taken me all week to make another one in my blacksmith shop. No one will take this sword from me!" Andrew Barry spoke with conviction.

As he nodded to his brother Richard, Andrew held his sword tighter. Richard pounded Andrew's shoulder in agreement.

"It is hard to know who to trust anymore," Papa said. "I heard that some sons are going against their fathers. The sons don't believe that King George should be telling us how to run our lives or demanding taxes from us. The fathers think they owe allegiance to the King of England.

It is just like when we were in Ireland. The British tried to be our masters then and tell us what to do. We came to America for freedom from tyranny. This land is mine, and I will fight for it with every breath in my body!"

The men gathered there agreed.

Andrew Barry went on, "We need to be careful who we talk to. There could be more betrayal from our neighbors. When I was in Charles Town at the Customs House, there was a lot of name-calling. Those loyal to the King were being called Tories. Those loyal to our world were called Whigs or Patriots. I like the name of Patriot."

Several men nodded that they liked the name Patriot, too. The men grouped closer together under the tree. Their children were playing close by, and the fathers did not want to frighten them today.

Robert Nesbitt, who served as an elder of the church with Andrew, interrupted. "It is 1777, and we have been fighting for our homes the whole time we have been here. We cannot rely on anyone else. It seems to be getting worse.

"Do you remember the battle at Ninety-Six? It was almost two years ago. That was the day that we saw neighbors fighting against neighbors. Who would have believed that would happen?"

Master Nesbitt shook his head at the memory, "Major Andrew Williamson continues to talk about firing at his neighbors for the first time. Many of them almost didn't get back from that battle because of the twenty-four inches of snow."

"All my life I have wanted to be a soldier," said Kate's brother, Thomas.

"I remember when Papa gave me my first rifle. It is hard to fight against our neighbors. Do you remember when those three men came from the Council of Safety in Charles Town? They wanted to be sure we would fight for the state against the British. I was glad to tell them of my allegiance to our country here."

Charles Moore looked at his son and smiled with pride.

Thomas clinched his fists. "What is the matter with some of our neighbors? I still get mad when I think about Thomas Fletchall who lives over there in the Fairforest community. I could not believe the stand that he took against us. He was the colonel of the local militia and still would not back down on his loyalty to the English king. Even now he keeps on entertaining Tories at his plantation. Maybe he has forgotten he lost all his public offices. His time in jail in Charles Town for backing the British didn't teach him anything."

As Papa tapped the end of his pipe on the tree, Kate called from the steps.

"Dinner is ready, gentlemen, when you are ready to eat."

The men left their worried faces and minds under the tree. They gathered with their wives and children in a circle in front of the house. Reverend Alexander thanked God for the food, prayed for each family, and asked God's blessing on their fight for independence from Britain's taxes and rule.

Patriot

After dinner everyone enjoyed the games. The men and women played tug-of-war. There were many hoop races among the children. Boys and girls raced on foot, and the men raced their horses. Kate was pleased when Andrew won the horse race. She heard Thomas talking about the race track he wanted to have at his farm one day. The Scots-Irish were proud of their horses. She also noticed that her brothers remembered the best hiding places she had shown them for hide-and-seek.

As many started to the house for lemonade or to the well for water, Master Penn began to play his fife. The song was familiar to everyone. Before long, their singing could be heard across the Tyger River.

*Yankee Doodle came to town*
*For to buy a firelock;*
*We will tar and feather him*
*And so we will John Hancock.*
*Yankee Doodle. keep it up,*
*Yankee Doodle Dandy,*
*Mind the music and the step,*
*And with the girls be handy.*
*Father and I went down to camp*
*Along with Captain Good'in*
*And there we see the men and boy as*
*As thick as hasty puddin'.*
*And there was Captain Washington,*
*And gentlefolks about him,*
*They say he's grown so tarnal proud,*

*He will not ride without them.*
*And there was Captain Washington*
*Upon a slapping stallion.*
*A giving orders to his men'*
*I guess there was a million.*
*Yankee Doodle, keep it up.*
*Yankee Doodle Dandy,*
*Mind the music and the step.*
*And with the girls be handy.*

One war was over, but another was brewing. The war with the British was headed south. The Scots-Irish were ready.

# 9

# A Scary Day

By now Kate and Andrew knew whom they could trust and whom they could not. Some of their neighbors believed they owed allegiance to King George III because he was the one who gave them their land grants. At Nicholls Mill or at Hannah's Cow Pens, arguments became a daily occurrence. The angry talk often led to fistfights and threats.

The British army moved closer and closer to the Upcountry. The summer of 1780 was like a civil war in the Upcountry with neighbor fighting neighbor, and sometimes, sons fighting their fathers.

The Tory bands destroyed crops and burned the houses of their Patriot neighbors. Then the Patriots attacked the Tory farms in revenge. Both sides had learned how effective an ambush could be. Every surprise attack brought about destruction.

Ever since the Waxhaw massacre sixty miles east of them on May 29, 1780, Patriot men and women fought even harder to defend themselves.

On that day British Colonel Banastre Tarleton, known as "Bloody Tarleton," defeated the Continental Army troops under Colonel Abraham Buford. He had refused quarter, or mercy, to the defeated Continental troops. He paid no attention to Colonel Buford's white flag of surrender. More than one hundred Patriots were killed. Now it only took a mention of Tarleton's name for people to clinch their fists in an angry response. "Remember Tarleton's Quarter" became the battle cry in the Upcountry.

On one morning in June, Kate moved the spinning wheel out on the porch to enjoy the warm weather. She usually kept the wheel near the fireplace in the keeping room. Kate enjoyed spinning. She could talk and work at the same time. Twisting the fibers into yarn on the wheel was second nature to her now. Weaving the yarn into the cloth on the loom was much harder work.

Kate knew she needed to use every bit of the wool. They couldn't get cloth from England anymore. She had to make all the cloth if they were going to have anything new.

Even with passing clothes down to the younger children, the clothes eventually wore out. Kate remembered her mama saying, "Waste not, want not." Kate was not wasteful.

Her four children were on the porch around her. One-year-old Katie was taking a nap in her cradle. Charles was building a tower with his blocks. Andrew had ordered them from England. All the children enjoyed them. Andrew was convinced that the blocks helped with learning the alphabet. There were pictures on both sides. The words for the pictures were written in English on one side and in Latin on the other side.

As a three-year-old, Charles always laughed with glee when he knocked them over. He then would start building again. Charles paid no attention to the English and Latin words on the blocks. One day he would start asking what the words meant.

John, at age nine, was very serious about everything. Kate worried about his seriousness. He was always listening for something. In fact, he often carefully raised his head and looked around him to see what was going on. She presumed it was because his whole life had revolved around war.

It wasn't just the wilderness where they lived that was dangerous. There had always been the danger of battles with the Cherokee or Tories near the river or in their own backyards. John was taught as a toddler to run and hide at his parents' commands. Andrew would tolerate no disobedience to this rule.

John whittled with the knife his father gave him now. He was very careful with that knife. His carving was precise and accurate. Kate prayed he would not have to use that knife to defend himself one day. He was too young.

Kate couldn't believe that Polly would be six in September. Polly was playing church with her doll. Earlier she played school. Kate knew that the next game would be house. Then she might have a tea party, and Kate and the dolls would be invited. Listening to Polly's imagination was a joy. She was so creative.

"Why does Papa call you Peggy, Mama?" asked John. "No one else calls you that.

We all call you Mama. Grandpa Charles calls you Katie sometimes. All my uncles and aunts call you Kate. Why do you have so many names? Everyone just calls me John."

Kate was constantly surprised at the questions her oldest son asked. She continued to spin as she answered him.

"It is not a secret, John. When your Papa came courting, he asked me one day if he could call me Peggy. I told him that was fine, and he calls me that to this day."

"When will Papa lead his militia home? Isn't it time for his men to serve as the home guards? Since he is the Captain, I think he should do that. They have been out patrolling the roads and rivers long enough," persisted John.

"I know! I know!" shouted his younger sister, Polly. "Grandpa Charles told me that Papa and his men had to take turns playing soldiers. Sometimes they guard us and the farms. Sometimes they go check on the forts. And sometimes they fight in real battles. It's not Papa's turn to be home and guard us."

Polly's eyes became bigger and bigger as she told all she knew about the militia.

Quickly John said, "Polly, will you bowl with

me? I will let you be first. Let me get those Tory soldiers. Our bowling balls need to knock them down a peg or two."

Kate smiled as she saw how protective John was of his younger sister. She would tell him later how proud she was of him. Now they were busy playing as she tried to finish her work.

Suddenly Kate heard the sounds of horses' hoofs and men's whoops in the distance. She pushed Katie's cradle in the door and told the children to get behind her.

Her musket was right beside her, and she picked it up. Kate noticed John pick up his knife and hold it behind his back.

Andrew had warned her before he left this time that she must be more vigilant.

Charles Town had fallen to the British on May 12. The British general, Sir Henry Clinton, had taken the city in his second attempt. Then Colonel Buford lost at the Battle of Waxhaws. Andrew was right with his counsel. The fighting had finally reached the Upcountry, and it was headed for their home.

"John," said Kate earnestly, leaning down to look him in the eyes, "No matter what happens, your job is to take care of the younger children. I know I can depend on you. They are so little, and they need you."

"Mama! Mama! Why are those men hollering at us?" the panicked Polly interrupted.

Polly tried to bury herself in Kate's skirt.

As Kate put her arm around Polly, she said to

John, "Please promise me that you will protect them. Don't worry about me; just keep them safe. John, do you hear me? Will you promise me that?"

Suddenly John turned from his mama to pick up Charles as the three-year-old walked toward the steps of the porch. John handed the child two of his blocks and set him down again.

The men rode along the fence getting closer to the house every second. Their voices were louder. Now even Charles was looking afraid because of the noise the horsemen were making. Kate gave Polly a quick hug and told the child she must stay behind her skirts close to John.

Kate then took a deep breath and said to her oldest child, "I know you always keep your promises to me. Your papa has taught you that a man's word is his bond. You would never break your word. I need to hear you promise me that you will do this."

"I will always protect them, Mama," John said softly.

Eight horsemen galloped toward the porch. They ran their horses right through her herb garden. The soldiers continued to holler even after they reached the house. Shooting their rifles in the air, a couple of them even raced around the house. They finally lined up in front of the steps. Kate pointed the musket from one soldier to another. Without a word, she looked each one in the eye. She recognized two of the men immediately.

After he jumped off his horse, Master Elliott bowed arrogantly. There was condemnation in his voice. He was a Tory.

"Missus, you can just put that musket down. I need to speak to your husband."

Kate's voice was firm. "My husband is not here." She did not put the musket down.

Master Elliott turned to his men. "Did ye' hear that, gentlemen? The little wife says her husband is not here." They all laughed.

John tried to step around his mother, but Kate said firmly, "No, John."

He reluctantly obeyed.

Kate still had not lowered the musket. There were tears falling down Polly's cheeks. She started to shake. John stiffly stood by his mother. Master Elliott climbed the steps to the porch. His men were now silent.

"Missus, I need for you to tell me where your husband is," Elliott said. "We have important business to discuss with him. It will go hard for you and your young'uns if you won't tell me where I can find him."

The rest of Elliott's men climbed off their horses. Suddenly Elliott knocked Kate's musket out of her hands and up into the air. It fell over the porch.

Charles screamed, "Mama! Mama!" He ran and hit Elliott on the knee with one of his blocks. Elliott picked the three-year-old up and handed him off to one of his men.

"I will make you talk, Missus. Now, tell me where your husband and that sorry lot of men he leads are." Elliott grabbed Kate's arms as he spoke. "Roger, bring me that rope out of my saddlebags."

He swung Kate around and tied her arms. He almost knocked her over, but John helped her stay upright. Both Polly and Charles were crying now.

"Don't hurt my mama! Oh, please, sir, don't hurt my mama!" shouted Polly.

"I will give you one more chance, Missus," threatened Elliott. "If you don't answer me then, I will thrash you until you do."

"John," Kate said loudly. "Don't forget your promise to me!"

Elliott hit Kate. Then he hit her again. He looked for some response from Kate. There was none. And he hit Kate again. All three children screamed at him to stop. Two of the soldiers looked in disbelief at what Elliott had done, but they said nothing. Kate also said nothing.

"You are just as stubborn as your old man," screamed Elliott. "I will find that traitor! I don't need any information from you. I will find him myself. Come on, men. Let's get out of here. We have the King's business to take care of. Those dirty rebels can't be far away."

He stomped off the porch, put Charles down on the steps, and jumped on his mount. With more shooting of their rifles and cries of "Long live the King," the Tories galloped off the Barry property.

"Help me, John, to get free of these ropes. They are sorely hurting my arms," Kate said softly.

She sat down on the steps with Charles and

Polly in her lap and one arm around John. With tears running down her bruised face, she held her crying children for a long time.

# A Scout and a Spy

Kate became a scout and spy for Andrew's militia. She received messages and took the news to him. She knew all the Indian trails in the area. She learned those trails when they first moved to Carolina. Kate was never afraid to push her horse into a flooded creek to reach and warn Andrew that the British soldiers were near. She rode her horse, Dolly, from farm to farm to give each Patriot man the call to arms.

John begged every day to ride with her, but his parents refused.

On the morning of August 7, 1780, John came running from the woods near the house. "Mama! Mama! Master Penn hollered at me from across the river. Colonel Shelby needs all the militia units together to stop Ferguson's men. Another Patriot rode to the Penn farm with the news. We need to tell Papa and his men."

"I don't have time to saddle my horse, John," shouted Kate. "Run and get him from the barn for me."

John never stopped running. He knew this was

one way he could help protect his family. He was in and out of the barn as quick as water running off a duck's back. John talked to the horse as he led the mare to the house.

"Now, Dolly, you have to gallop as fast as you can. Take Mama to Papa's campsite. Here's an apple for you to start you on your way. You had a good rest last night, and I know you are ready for a good run. Those soldiers told us a sorry story about what keeps happening to our men. It is time to stand our ground and not let those Tories take over. We can drive the British out of Carolina!

"Dolly, you can help Mama get the word to Papa and his men. You need to run your very fastest. You bring Mama back quickly, and I will have you some extra oats for supper."

Kate threw her bonnet on her head. She grabbed the socks she finished knitting for Andrew the night before. She ran to meet John at the mounting block. John held the reins for his mother. Then he gave Dolly one last pat, and the two took off.

She knew the quickest way to Andrew's camp was across her Papa's land and over the river. Dolly knew the way to her parents' home. All Kate did was encourage the horse to gallop faster.

As they traveled, Kate thought about the travellers who had stopped at their home two days ago. They knew it was safe to stop because of the lighted Betty lamp in the window.

They had news that brought tears to Kate's eyes. She could hardly think about it even now and dreaded telling Andrew about it.

As Kate grew closer to the campsite, she gave the secret whistle to alert the guards along the pickets. Those camp guards had been known to take a pot shot at a friend who forgot to give the signal. Kate was greeted with smiles and waves from the fifteen men with Andrew.

She immediately saw her husband cleaning his rifle. When she arrived at his side, he helped her dismount.

"Two bits of news for you," said Kate. "A scout from Colonel Isaac Shelby sent word that he needs all available militia to muster with his men. Patrick Ferguson and his men are headed toward Cedar Springs."

"Thanks, my darling," answered Andrew. "What was the other piece of news?"

"Oh, Andrew, two days ago some of our men came by on their way to check on their farms. They stopped for the night and slept in the barn. Their stories were of the many Patriot homes and farms being destroyed. Women and children are without shelter. They are even hanging old men and burning churches. Will it never end, Andrew?"

"Yes, it will end, and the British will run back to England! Our cause is just, Kate. We are winning the skirmishes, and the defeat in Charles Town is behind us. We are committed. We must fight, and we will fight to win," Andrew assured his wife.

Andrew's men heard Kate's reports and his response. They cheered and threw their hats in the air. They were ready to follow their captain

Sentry

that minute. For five years Americans had fought against the British. These citizen soldiers in the Upcountry believed that the British defeat was only a skirmish away.

As Andrew helped Kate mount the mare again, he cautioned and said, "Hurry back to the house now in case any enemy units detour toward our farm again. This is not a safe time out on the trails. We can be ready shortly to move out."

He turned to Thomas to give the word to the men to break camp and prepare to move out.

As Kate took the reins from Andrew, she turned to him again, "We must fight harder! We can't let the British take our land away. I remember Papa talking to us when we were children about why he came to America in the first place. He still believes God blessed him and gave his family their freedom here in the Upcountry."

Kate watched Andrew's back straighten as he answered her. "Your father is right, my dear. God trusted us with the land to begin with. He will help us protect it. We won't despair over a little bad news. I love you, Peggy. I will see you soon."

Andrew turned and ran for his horse.

# War on the Home Front

"Wake up, John," whispered Kate. "Remember you are going with me today to hide the supplies for the militia."

John had slept in his clothes, so he was ready quickly. He rubbed his eyes several times as he splashed water on his face from the pitcher in the bedroom.

"I'm ready, Mama," John said, as he met her on the front porch. "I'll go saddle the horses."

Kate had packed the knapsacks the night before. John jumped over them before he ran down the steps toward the barn. He could not believe that Papa was going to let him ride with Mama today to hide more supplies.

Papa was almost recovered from the gunshot wound to his leg. Even though Papa was wounded at the Battle at Musgrove Mill, he was ready to get back to his men. The doctor said Papa might limp the rest of his life, but John didn't think so. Papa was a determined man. He had already thrown away the cane he had been using.

Papa had talked to John a lot while he was

Musgrove Mill

recuperating. Father and son played many games of chess together on the porch. While they played, Andrew taught John the rules of strategy necessary to win at chess. Papa answered all of John's questions about how to plan an ambush. Andrew also explained why it was so important to obey orders. He told John details about some of the battles he had fought in. He had never talked about those battles before.

John told Dolly as he cinched her saddle, "Papa trusts me, Dolly. He knows I can do my part."

When the horses were saddled, Kate and John raced each other down the dirt road toward the river. They were both anxious to carry out their jobs to help the soldiers.

In the holes of trees and in stumps Kate and John hid pouches full of corn and gourds of well water for Andrew's men. They also left cloth bags of dried apples and raisins. Kate made the bags out of scraps of cloth and tied them shut with leather. Sometimes forest animals found the hiding places, but most of the time they didn't. Several times, men had told Kate those extra supplies gave them just enough food and energy to make it back home.

Kate also tucked a few letters for the men from their families in those trees and stumps. One wife gave Kate a care package with her husband's name on it. John made sure that package was thoroughly hidden. No one in the militia would open another soldier's mail or package, but the Tories would. Andrew's men respected each other's privacy.

At one of the secret places, they picked up a letter from a soldier for his wife and children. Kate made sure that letter was delivered before she and John went home at the end of the day. Kate knew how excited she was to find a letter from Andrew at one of the drops, so she wasted no time with those special deliveries.

Andrew and his men appreciated all Kate did to help them survive that summer and fall of 1780. It was a very dangerous time. They knew she took many chances to keep them informed of the enemy's whereabouts and keep them in touch with their families. The Tory bands were everywhere in the Upcountry. If the Tories caught her, they might shoot her. They had shot other scouts.

The men were willing to do without the comforts of home for days on end to fight for freedom. They knew independence from the tyranny of England depended on their pledge of allegiance to their new country. Kate had made that same pledge.

Mother and son rode together long hours that day. John was excited to be helping Kate. They were tired when they returned home that evening, but John was proud to ride with his mama as a scout and soldier.

The next week came all too quickly. Andrew left again to join his men. Life settled back in the routine of a house without Papa. John did most of the outside chores alone again. He milked the cows twice a day. He plowed the winter garden. Wood had to be cut daily for the fireplace. There were fences to be mended and tools to be sharpened.

John hunted for fresh meat and fished in the Tyger River. The horses had to be groomed and the barns cleaned. John guarded the house, too. His rifle was always close by. John missed his papa. It was hard to do it all alone.

There was a feeling of constant tension on the Barry farm. Even Polly and Charles were jumpy and nervous. There were daily news reports of more burned fields and homes. The Tories stole animals and supplies from farms, leaving families destitute They had no qualms at putting women and children out of their homes with no shelter, and they were ruthless in shooting Patriots they encountered.

As Kate walked toward the apple trees on a late Wednesday morning in November to gather the last apples for a pie, she heard shouts and gunfire in the distance coming from across the river near her parents' home two miles away. She knew she needed to get word to Andrew immediately and ran to the barn. Dolly's bridle was hanging right by the door. Kate threw it over the horse's head. In just minutes, the two were out of the barn and on the trail to the camp.

Andrew and his men were on a patrol of the area. Kate reined Dolly in as she heard her husband's whistle.

When she could see his face, she hollered, "I heard shouts and gunfire coming from across the river!"

Kate moved her horse off the trail as Andrew and his militia raced by. Andrew responded to

Kate with a wave and a smile. There was no time for words. Then Kate started back home to be sure everything was all right there. The sound of gunshots didn't stop for almost a half an hour.

It was hard for Kate and the children to wait for news. Andrew had been adamant in his rule that they should not leave the house for any reason when they could hear the sounds of fighting. His rules were for their protection.

Kate decided to put Katie down for her afternoon nap. Katie had a difficult time going to sleep. As she rocked Katie, Kate started singing. It was a song that all her children knew.

*Sleep my child and peace attend thee,*
*All through the night.*
*Guardian angels God will send thee,*
*All through the night.*
*Soft the drowsy hours are creeping.*
*Hill and vale in slumber sleeping,*
*I my loving vigil keeping*
*All through the night.*

*While the moon her watch is keeping,*
*All through the night.*
*While the weary world is sleeping,*
*All through the night.*
*O'er thy spirit gently stealing,*
*Visions of delight revealing,*
*Breathes a pure and holy feeling*
*All through the night.*

*Love, to thee my thoughts are turning*
*All through the night.*
*All for thee my heart is yearning,*
*All through the night.*
*Though sad fate our lives may sever*
*Parting will not last forever,*
*There's a hope that leaves me never,*
*All through the night.*

Finally Katie slept. John entertained Polly and Charles by playing with the wooden Noah's Ark set that Grandpa Charles had made for them. While Kate dusted again the furniture that she had just dusted that morning, she prayed for the safety of Andrew and his men. The windows and doors remained shuttered and barred until they heard Andrew's whistle and his voice later that afternoon.

John helped his mother take the wooden bar off the front door. They all greeted Andrew at the bottom of the porch steps. Kate searched Andrew's face for any bad news.

She sighed with relief when she saw his half-smile. Within minutes the family was in front of the fireplace listening to Andrew tell the story of their skirmish with a band of Tories.

"The Tories were headed for your papa's home, Kate. We ambushed them close to the river and started shooting before we even jumped off our horses."

Polly interrupted, "Did you have your extra bullets in your mouth, Papa? John told me all the soldiers keep extra bullets in their mouths, so they can reload quickly. He said you don't get thirsty either. I don't think bullets would taste too good."

Andrew and Kate both laughed. It helped to break the tension. Their children were certainly not learning about war just from books. They were living right in the middle of one. Their questions were always thoughtful and based on experience.

"Yes, Polly. I had the extra bullets in my mouth. And you are right. Bullets just don't compare to your mama's shortbread." Andrew took Polly on his lap as he spoke.

"Those Tories lined up across the Indian trail just like the British army does. We had time to reload again before they ever got in formation. We made some good shots before they started shooting back."

The children were quiet and listened intently to their father. They wanted to know the rest of his story.

"We kept on shooting until the Tories retreated. There was so much smoke that I couldn't see the end of my musket. It was tense for a bit, but our surprise attack helped. I guess we learned the importance of ambushes during the war with the Cherokee."

Andrew was silent and looked in the fire. Kate saw both anger and sorrow in his blue eyes. She looked at her son John's face and saw the same anger and sorrow. The war took daily determination to defend their homes. Kate saw her son growing up to be a man before his time.

# CHRISTMAS DAY, 1780

"I caught another one, John. That one was almost too big for my mouth. Some of it splattered on my nose!" exclaimed Polly. She wanted so badly to beat her big brother at something.

"Can we make snow cream when we get back tonight?" asked Polly.

"I want cream," chimed Charles.

"I'll bring in the clean snow, Mama," added John.

Kate and Andrew spoke at the same time, "Yes, we can do that."

The snow was about three inches deep on the ground. The small flakes had started the afternoon before. Polly and John continued to try to catch the snowflakes with their tongues. Katie was also trying, but she wasn't having much success. All three laughed as they enjoyed the first snowfall.

Kate put her baskets of food in the wagon. She had made shortbread to share with their friends on Christmas. Unlike Protestants in Europe, the Scots-Irish in America did not mark the beginning of Christmas Day with the firing of guns at dawn.

There was no Yule Log nor any talk of the Twelve Days of Christmas. Evergreens were not brought in to decorate the homes. Foxhunts, dancing balls, and late night dinners for many guests were not scheduled. None of these traditions were kept by the Scots-Irish who settled in the Upcountry. They typically spent Christmas day quietly, going about their daily tasks and going to the meeting house. They celebrated quietly, but Kate still wanted the other families in their congregation to know that she and Andrew appreciated their friendship.

Kate used her mother's recipe for shortbread. There were only three ingredients: butter, flour, and sugar.

*Shortbread Cookie Recipe*

*1 cup sugar*
*2 cups butter*
*3 cups flour*
*Blend all ingredients and bake until*
*golden brown in moderate oven.*

Kate had made the butter and planted the wheat for the flour. Nowadays she didn't make butter everyday in her churn, because they didn't have as many cows as they once did. Some had been stolen; others ran off.

Their wheat crop had been mostly destroyed by a band of Tories that rode through their fields. So Kate was not using her mill stone as much either this year. Milling the wheat for flour was not really a job she missed. It was hard work turning that mill stone.

The sugar cone was almost gone, too. She knew she might run out by the end of the month. Before the war, a trader from Charles Town had come to the Upcountry almost every week. Kate could always buy a sugar cone wrapped in paper. She would cut off what she needed and buy another when she ran out. There was no telling when another trader would come by with more sugar or anything else for her to buy.

Kate remembered how much Mama enjoyed baking her communion cakes for her neighbors as a surprise. This year Kate really enjoyed making the shortbread. She understood now why her mama smiled when she packed up her communion cakes to give away. It was fun to surprise friends and family with gifts.

"Mama, did you get all the bags of shortbread we made?" asked Polly. She jumped up and down trying to see inside the baskets.

"Yes, Polly, I believe I have them all. Every family in the church will get a bag today. Did I thank you for helping me make the cookies?" asked Kate.

"Oh, yes, Mama, you thanked me. You told me I was the best helper and the sweetest girl in the whole wide world," Polly smiled.

Kate smiled as she gave the six-year-old a big hug.

The night before, the family had worked together to tie a sprig of holly berries and leaves to each cloth bag full of cookies. Andrew told stories about his years growing up with his brothers. His children always enjoyed hearing about his childhood. They all drank apple cider and taste-tested the shortbread. They enjoyed their family night together; it was a good evening.

Before the children went to bed, they wanted to sing. It was John's turn to choose a song they all knew. Andrew took his fiddle from the case.

"Let's sing a Christmas song, Papa. I like 'While Shepherds Watched Their Flocks.' You said your grandpapa was a shepherd in Ireland."

As the family sang the last verse, Kate and Andrew wondered if peace would be part of their new year.

*All glory be to God on high,*
*And to the Earth be peace;*
*Good will henceforth from heaven to men*
*Begin and never cease*
*Begin and never cease.*

On the way to Sunday services at Nazareth Presbyterian Church, John rode his own horse. Polly, Charles, and Katie rode in the wagon with Kate. Andrew was home on leave from his unit, and he led the way. John was so proud to be riding a horse, rather than walking or riding in the wagon.

Andrew took his responsibility as elder in the church very seriously. An elder was elected by other elders. He had to be a man of good reputation. Part of an elder's job was to help rule the church and assist the pastor. Andrew tried to make good decisions. A Presbyterian elder also had the responsibility of leading a Scots-Irish militia unit. That was why Andrew was the captain of his unit.

Andrew never missed going to church on a Sunday, unless he was with his unit out on patrol or fighting with his men. Robert Nesbitt, John Mucklewrath, and Thomas Peden were the other elders at Nazareth. They would all be at services today. The four men had often said that they were glad no Tory families were in their congregation.

Reverend Joseph Alexander was their pastor. He had been with them since the spring of 1772. He was a learned man. He encouraged his congregation every Sunday to be obedient to God, read their Bibles, and to help others. The congregation traditionally celebrated the Lord's Supper twice a year – once in the spring and once in the fall. After those services, they always took up extra money for the poor.

Reverend Alexander had announced the previous Sunday that the congregation was going to have an extra Lord's Supper service today. He encouraged everyone to be there for this special Christmas celebration.

As the Barry family traveled through the snow, Andrew listened intently for any suspicious sounds. Daily they heard news of more skirmishes between Patriots and Tories. Even a ride to church services could be dangerous now.

British
Soldier

A scout had come to the Barry home the day before from the village of Ninety-Six. The scout had news about another battle near Long Cane. More Patriots had died. He and the other elders would need to discuss it after services today. They needed to analyze every bit of intelligence from every scout.

Andrew believed they needed another victory like the one at King's Mountain in October. That victory gave all of the Upcountry the assurance that they really could beat the British. The Patriots needed that boldness again.

The children talked and laughed as they traveled through the woods. Their thoughts were on snow, and Andrew's were on war.

Andrew remembered the last words of the sermon by Samuel Doak at the Sycamore Shoals muster before that battle at King's Mountain. His words became the soldiers' battle cry that day. Andrew remembered he and his men shouting together "for the sword of the Lord and Gideon" as they ambushed the troops of Patrick Ferguson.

Major Ferguson had around eleven hundred troops under his command, outnumbering the Patriots by two hundred men. The Patriots won, and they could do it again. They just needed to be reminded!

After the church service, the four elders gathered to talk about the latest news. They moved to the back corner of the church. Privacy was necessary to talk about military matters. The men quickly put behind them the Patriot defeat at Long Cane. They focused on how to win the next skirmish.

"We need to gather all the information we can from every scout," Andrew thoughtfully said. "Do you remember all the scouts that helped us with information at King's Mountain? Even though we marched through pouring rain overnight, our leaders knew exactly where to find Patrick Ferguson and his troops the next day."

Thomas Penn leaned forward eagerly to share his recollections of that October 7th afternoon. Andrew motioned for him to go ahead.

"I heard tell it was the scout and spy Joseph Kerr who brought that information to Major William Campbell," added Master Penn.

"Joseph has been crippled since birth. He has certainly not used his physical challenges as an excuse not to be part of this fight for independence," John Mucklewrath said. "Joseph can't even walk without his crutch. Those British and Tories just don't seem to recognize him as a possible threat. They speak of all manner of military matters around him. Then he brings the news to us. He has made his physical weakness into a strength. What a brave soldier and Patriot Joseph is!"

There was a building excitement in their voices as the four continued to talk.

Robert Nesbitt quickly responded, "Yes, and our leaders found out Ferguson had sent men to find food, too, so his force was weaker on that afternoon. Didn't the scouts say that over a hundred men were sent on that foraging expedition? If we had waited, the outcome might have been different."

Andrew nodded his head in agreement.

"Do you remember how it rained all day and all night before we attacked?" reminded Thomas Penn. "Those Tories weren't expecting us to attack so quickly. I wish we could have seen their faces more clearly when we started hollering! Those war whoops we learned during the Indian wars can make the hair stand up on your head."

Thomas shivered as he remembered making those war cries. He hoped his children never heard hollers like that. He looked over his shoulder and smiled at them safely playing in another corner.

Andrew continued, "I was glad to be put in the trees as a marksman. Up in those trees, it was just like shooting at a flock of turkeys. I wanted some revenge on the Tories after one of them wounded me at Musgrove Mill."

"Have you heard the song that has been written about the battle at King's Mountain?" Master Penn asked. "My sons came in from the field singing it the other day. It tells our story quite well. I don't remember all the words, but it ended like this. 'To all the brave regiments, Let's toast them for their health, And may our good country, Have quietude and wealth.' We could use a little quiet in this new country of ours."

The four elders shook hands with each other. They walked to the altar at the front of the church and placed money in the offering plate to help the many needy families in their community. Then they put on their hats, went outside, and joined their families. Reminiscing about the great victory at King's Mountain firmed their resolve once again that the British would be defeated.

When good-byes were said, the families set off down the trails. They wanted to get home before dark. The light snow continued to fall in the Upcountry that Christmas Day in 1780.

# THE BATTLE
# AT THE COW PENS, 1781

Andrew folded the small piece of paper and carefully placed it in the hollow of his quill pen. For two years now Andrew and Kate had used this method to get messages to each other. There was a dead tree close to the river that they used as a dropping off point. It was close enough to their house for Kate to check it every day.

He needed to get this information to Kate immediately. She would pass the news at once to the Patriots living around the Tyger River.

Just minutes before, another scout had arrived. He had shouted this message before riding on: "General Daniel Morgan is at Grindall Shoals on the banks of the Pacolet River. Militia units are joining him. All the Patriots need to join him as soon as possible. This time we are going to stop those British and throw them out of our country for good!"

Andrew took the message back out of the quill and added,

*My dearest Kate,*

*I look with much pleasure toward the next day
of seeing you and our children.*

*With much love and gratitude,
Andrew*

A couple of hours later, Kate left the house to check the dead tree for a message. In case anyone was watching the house, she gathered some kindling as she walked. She quickly took the quill pen into the house to read it.

She gasped as she read Andrew's message. Kate knew she had to leave now. The children had spent the night with their grandparents. If she didn't get home for a while, John and Polly could take care of Charles and Katie.

Kate did not wait to saddle her horse. She wasted no time in getting on the trail either. She raced from one farm to another to spread the word that the Patriots were needed by General Daniel Morgan.

The winter rains had set in, and the roads were nothing but mud. Often Kate's horse slid and almost lost her balance on the wet leaves. Once a tree limb caught the hood of her cloak and pulled it off her face. The icy rain ran down her back. Kate did not even slow down. The waters of the Tyger River were high, and the wind buffeted them both as the horse swam across. They still made it in record time.

Both the men and the women of the Upcountry knew General Morgan's reputation. He was respected and known for his bravery. This famous rifleman had proved himself in combat as a leader. He was a hero at the Battle of Saratoga, and the Patriots were excited he was here. They trusted him to finally put an end to the unwanted British presence in South Carolina.

Lord Cornwallis also had respect for the new military leadership in South Carolina. The British commander had his spies all over the Upcountry to check on General Morgan and Major General Nathaniel Greene. He knew the reputation and fame of both soldiers.

Cornwallis had made his headquarters in Winnsboro about sixty-five miles from the Upcountry. He decided to split his forces in half to go after both generals. Cornwallis chose Lt. Colonel Banastre Tarleton to go after General Morgan. Tarleton had an army of over one thousand men.

General Morgan had only five hundred men in his force. General Greene called them the Flying Army. The traveled on good mounts with little equipment, and they knew the territory well. Their mission was to cut off the British supply lines. Colonel Andrew Pickens added strength to General Morgan's forces. He took his Long Cane militia of one hundred fifty men to join General Morgan's men on January 4, 1781.

Because of Colonel Pickens' reputation, the General put Colonel Pickens in command of the

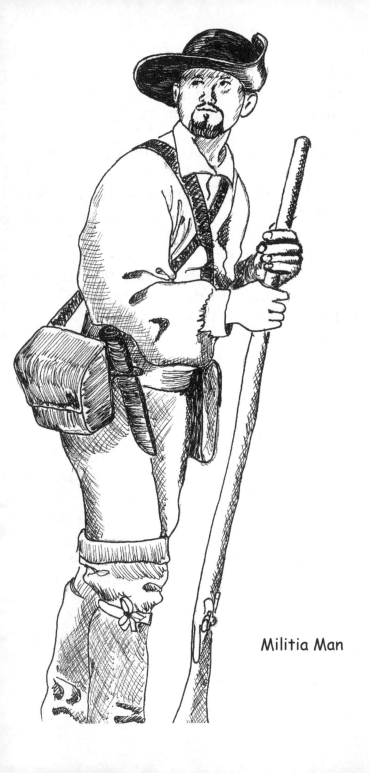

Militia Man

militia.

Still they needed more men. Scouts went out all over the Upcountry with the message that more soldiers were needed immediately. Kate was one of those scouts.

Every Patriot unit in the Upcountry responded. No one chose to stay behind.

Those militiamen left their homes and families once again. Around five hundred of them moved out on horseback. Each carried his rifle. They met General Morgan and Colonel Pickens at the Cow Pens. The Scots-Irish had resolve in their hearts that they would fight to their last breath. They were hungry for a victory.

After Kate finished her route that day, she raced back home to check on her children. When she came around the bend, she saw a candle in the window of the keeping room. What a welcome sight it was to see that small light shining from her home! Kate knew everything was fine.

She hurried her tired horse to the stable and ran to the house shouting, "Hello! Hello! Anyone home?"

The door opened, and there stood her parents. Her mother was holding Katie. John, Polly, and Charles were right behind them. Kate's two youngest brothers, Andrew and Charlie, were there, too.

There was much confusion, as they all tried to talk at once. Finally Mama Mary urged everyone inside by the fire. Kate really didn't want to do anything but hold her children.

"Now, tell me quickly what happened," said Kate. "I can't wait another minute!

Why are all of you here?"

Papa Charles began the story. "John and Polly were going to ride back home together on John's horse this morning. We were going to bring the younger two later. Polly sprained her ankle jumping off the porch after breakfast. We had her soak her ankle in some warm water. Your mama put some rosemary oil in the water to take out the swelling."

Polly pulled up her dress to show Kate her ankle. "See, Mama, it is so much better. Mama Mary is just as good a doctor as you are!"

Kate smiled at her daughter and thanked her mother.

John took up telling the story next. "After Polly soaked her foot, Papa Charles put her up behind me on my horse for us to come home. Polly couldn't keep her ankle from hitting the horse. She cried, so Papa Charles brought her here in the wagon."

"And when we got home, you weren't here, Mama," continued Polly.

"Mama, it's so cold outside. Where were you?" asked four-year-old Charles.

Kate picked him up. "I had to take an important message to your papa's friends, Charles. I am glad you were safe with Papa Charles and Mama Mary while I was gone."

"Mama and Papa, will you and the boys spend the night with us, please? The weather is just frightful. It is getting colder by the hour, and there seems to be some sleet mixed in with the rain now," said Kate.

"We would be delighted to stay, Kate. It will give us more time with you and the children. I want to hear your news also," answered her papa.

Three days later the women and children of the Nazareth congregation went to Andrew Coan's house to wait for news of the battle at the Cow Pens. His house was nearest the meeting house. The children played. The women prayed. They knew their husbands and fathers were in harm's way because Tarleton was on his way to attack General Morgan's forces. Over one thousand militia and Continental soldiers awaited Tarleton and his troops on January 17, 1781 on the muddy Green River Road.

Some of the women started to make a new quilt. Others were putting a meal together. No one could sit still. Finally Kate could stand it no longer. They could hear the cannons firing from far away, and she had to know what was happening.

Kate took her horse out again in that wintry weather. This time they only went as far as the shoals near Nicholls Mill. Because of the muddy bank, Dolly slid twice going down the hill. Kate gave the horse free reign, and she gained her balance.

When the two made it safely to the river, Kate tied her horse to a tree. There was a sheen of sleet on the rocks. Kate noticed sleet was on the wheel of the mill, too. Over the sound of the water, Kate heard more clearly the sounds of the cannons. Kate stood still for a while and prayed for the safety of those Patriot men and for their victory over the British.

It was too cold to stand still long. Kate went closer to the mill for shelter from the wind. Then she paced from rock to rock to try to stay warm. The wind blew some of the icy water up in her face, but she wiped it impatiently aside. Finally she stood quietly on the largest rock nearest the mill, the one that went out into the river. Kate intently gazed toward the sounds of war in the east and wondered about the outcome of the battle.

She heard the horse and rider before she saw him. He was whooping and crashing his horse through the woods. She recognized his voice. It was her neighbor, William Caldwell.

As soon as he saw her on the rocks, he reined his horse in from the gallop. He then headed for the other side of the river where Kate was.

"It was a glorious victory, Kate. It was a rout," shouted William. He pulled so hard on his horse's reins that the horse reared up on his hind legs. William just kept on grinning.

"We won! We did it! Tarleton escaped with a few of his cavalry. He ran from us, Mistress Barry! But we took five hundred prisoners. We whipped back that British army in only an hour!" he exclaimed. William Caldwell was talking so quickly that his words ran together.

"And what of my husband, Andrew, Master Caldwell? Is he safe?" Kate anxiously shouted.

William Caldwell then raced into the cold water of the Tyger River to get closer to her before he answered Kate's question. He was still smiling.

"I am happy to report to you, Mistress Barry, that I had the distinct honor of shaking hands with Captain Barry after the battle was over. He and your brother Thomas both fought bravely in the battle. I am proud to serve with them," he answered.

Kate, a most courageous daughter of the American Revolution, smiled and laughed in return. "What a glorious victory indeed, Master Caldwell. Let's go tell the other wives right now!"

Nichols Mill

# The Endless War

It was November of 1781, and the family already needed extra firewood. Andrew and his son John brought a dead tree closer to the house. John led the horse by the bridle, and the horse pulled the tree with a rope. Andrew watched to be sure the rope didn't get tangled with any stumps. The tree was long, and they would get a lot of firewood out of it. Andrew had to leave the next morning to join his militia unit. The two had been working hard to get many chores completed before Andrew left. He departed that night.

Even though the battle had been won at Cow Pens, the residents of the Upcountry still were not safe. "Bloody Bill" Cunningham had started making raids in the area. Cunningham was a Tory who had deserted the American cause to fight for the British.

Cunningham was vengeful in his attacks. He burned fields and homes. His men stole animals and supplies from the farms, and he was ruthless in his shooting of any Patriots. All the families were nervous as they continued with their daily lives.

A Patriot named Captain Steadman had been wounded in one of the skirmishes and was recuperating nearby at Charles and Mary Moore's home. Kate's sister Elizabeth had ridden over the day before to give the report that he was not healing well.

As Kate swept her front porch that day, she heard shouts and gunfire in the distance. The sounds were coming from the direction of her parents' home two miles away across the river. She needed to go tell Andrew, and there was no one to take care of Katie. She was close to panic.

John was certainly responsible enough, but he had gone rabbit hunting. Polly and Charles had begged to go, and Kate at last had given her permission. She had almost called the younger two back as she watched them march proudly

"Katie"

behind their brother with the haversacks over their shoulders. They would be back soon, but they were not at home now when she needed them to watch the baby.

As Kate came into the master bedroom, Katie walked toward her and asked to be picked up. She had been asleep taking her morning nap. Because she was two, Katie slept in the trundle bed now.

Katie was ready to play. "Mama, me up. Me up, now, please." She smiled sweetly as she reached both arms up toward Kate.

With a smile of greeting on her face, Kate leaned down to pick up her youngest.

"You are one beautiful girl, Katie, darling," said Kate. "I am so glad to see you. Did you have a most bonny nap this morning? Let me brush your hair a wee bit. You must have been rolling all over your bed."

Kate moved quickly, but quietly, so as not to frighten her daughter. She knew what she had to do.

After seeing to Katie's needs, Kate pulled the quilt off her bed. She spread it out on the floor and put pillows on it. Then she put Katie's favorite rag doll, some blocks, and the Noah's Ark set on the quilt. She hummed and talked to Katie as she made a special play space for her. Kate carried her daughter on her hip when she went to the kitchen to get a snack. Katie loved shortbread and dried apples. Her mama put some apple cider in Katie's two-handled cup for her. Today had to be a morning of favorite things for Katie!

Carrying Katie and balancing the cup and plate, Kate hurried back to the bedroom. She placed Katie on the quilt, as she kept talking. Then she picked up the heavy bedpost and gently placed it down on the corner of Katie's dress. For extra insurance, Kate wrapped one of her own large aprons around her daughter and tied the strings in a knot around the bedpost. Her mama and papa's big bed was going to be Katie's babysitter for the morning.

"I fancy that you are going to have a fine tea party until your brother and sister arrive," said Kate. "And your dolly is here to share it with you. It will be so much fun. I will be back ever so quickly. You can tell me about your fun time then, my precious angel. Will you give me a big kiss and tell Mama bye-bye?"

Kate hugged her daughter again and again. She covered the child's face with kisses and told her how much she loved her. When Kate turned to run out the door, the smile on her face turned to tears. But Kate kept on going. She had no choice.

She ran to the barn, bridled her horse, and quickly raced down the trails to find Andrew and his men. It wasn't long before she heard the sounds of other horses' hoofs along the Tyger River. Kate slowed and eased off the trail, and shortly she saw Andrew in the lead of his men. They were moving fast. There was no time for words. Kate pointed in the direction of her parents' home, and the men urged their horses to go faster.

Kate sighed with relief and quickly turned

her horse toward home. There was urgency in Kate's riding until the very moment she reined the horse in at the mounting block and jumped to the ground. Her heart was pounding from fear. Kate still could not believe she had left her two-year-old home alone. She ran up the steps of her home calling Katie's name. Kate heard her baby crying for her mama, and in seconds Kate was in the house hugging her daughter.

"Oh, sweet girl, I am so proud of you! You played with your toys while you waited for Mama to get back. You didn't make any messes either with your juice and cookies. I missed you, Katie, and Mama is right here."

After releasing Katie from her bedpost, she sat down and rocked the toddler. Kate wiped the tears off both their faces.

It wasn't long before she heard the excited voices of John, Polly, and Charles. Kate and Katie met the three on the front porch. As Kate hustled them inside, she was so relieved to see them that she forgot to ask about the hunting expedition. Now she could breathe another sigh of relief that all her children were in the house with her.

Again John helped bar the doors and windows. Kate encouraged Polly and Charles to sit down and play house with Katie. Then John and Kate again checked the windows and doors for safety. He reloaded his rifle and set it by the front door. John put his pouch with the extra bullets on the floor beside the rifle. Kate sat down in her rocking chair with her musket on the floor beside her. She watched the front door.

And the family waited. They continued to hear shots, but finally quiet fell.

Andrew would be home again only when his mission was over. They intently listened for his whistle.

At last they heard the thunder of horses' hoofs, and within minutes, Andrew was in the house.

As Andrew hugged Kate, he quickly reassured his wife, "Your papa, mama, brothers, and sisters are all fine, honey. Everyone is safe!"

"Papa! Papa! I got a rabbit," interrupted Charles. Charles pulled on his papa's jacket.

Both Kate and Andrew turned to look at the four-year-old. The startled Andrew spoke first, "What do you mean? How many times have I told you that you are too young to go hunting? You are not to even touch a gun unless I give it to you!"

"He and Polly went with me today, Papa. They carried the haversacks like you let them do when they went with us the other week," explained John.

Andrew sat down in his chair by the fire. "Well, that makes me feel a lot better. You scared me for a minute, Charles." He picked up Charles and held his son in his lap closely.

"It was 'Bloody Bill' Cunningham and his men," he began. "A man was starting to set fire to your parents' house when we arrived! We started our whoops and firing, and he dropped the torch. Some immediately started running for their horses, but the others fired back. Cunningham was threatening all of his men with hanging if they didn't fight back.

"Elizabeth was standing at the window upstairs. She kept shouting, but I couldn't understand her words. The rifles made too much noise. We just kept on shooting until the Tories retreated. My men are the best soldiers, Kate; they just refuse to give up."

"You don't give up either, Papa," John said.

Andrew smiled his appreciation to his son.

"'Bloody Bill' got away. I saw him smiling as he raced ahead of his men," Papa said. "I am glad he is a Tory. I would hate to have a man like that fighting on our side."

He paused. "It is not all good news, Kate." Andrew looked directly at his wife.

"Cunningham ordered Captain Steadman murdered in his bed! They shot him. And the other two officers who were visiting him at the house were chased down and also shot. The man shows no mercy. Elizabeth was trying to tell us about the murders when she shouted from upstairs. How could anyone shoot a wounded man? "

Andrew shook his head in disbelief. "We will bury those three fine soldiers this afternoon.

"We tried mighty hard to save everyone today. I wish…I wish things could have been different."

Andrew was finally quiet. His family was quiet, too.

Then Andrew grabbed Kate's hands, "We will win, Peggy! I promise you that we'll win this battle for our independence!"

# Epilogue

The cost of citizenship was high in South Carolina. More than one hundred thirty battles were fought here during the Revolutionary War, more than in any other state. Though the Battle at Cowpens was a great victory, there were thirty-one more engagements—like the one at the Moores' farm—after "Bloody Bill" Cunningham and his three hundred men came up from Charleston to search out Patriots.

After the Battle of Guilford Courthouse on March 15, 1781, British General Charles Lord Cornwallis headed north and was ultimately defeated by General George Washington at the Battle of Yorktown on October 19, 1781. Rather than pursuing Cornwallis, General Nathaniel Greene marched his Continental troops into South Carolina, taking this state back from the British – one battle at a time. Militia led by Brigadier General Francis Marion, Lieutenant Colonel Light Horse Harry Lee, and General Thomas Sumter also continued to engage the enemy. It wasn't until December 14, 1782, that the British finally evacuated Charleston. A peace treaty was finally signed in September 1783.

Even though "Bloody Bill" Cunningham did not burn the Moores' home in his raid into the Upcountry, his troops inflicted much damage to other properties during the closing days of the War. He and his men were cruel and merciless to all Patriots. Though he was pursued, "Bloody Bill" eventually escaped to the West Indies and lived out his life there.

With all the action that took place during those last years of the war in the Upcountry, it is amazing that Kate lost no family members. Those three brave soldiers killed by Cunningham's troops were buried in the Walnut Grove cemetery.

After the war ended, Major Crawford, a friend of Andrew Barry's, encouraged Andrew to find the Tory named Elliot who struck Kate. Andrew and ten other men pursued Elliot. At the sight of the man who struck his wife, Andrew picked up a stool and beat him senseless to the floor. The angry husband then cried out, "I am satisfied! I will not take his life." As a former magistrate and as a Presbyterian elder, Andrew did not believe in murder.

Days of peace came slowly to Kate and Andrew's household. Instead of Tory soldiers racing toward her house, she finally saw the first trader with his loaded packhorses, a sign of normalcy to life in the Upcountry. He was a welcome sight for Kate.

It would have been a relief to not have Andrew packing his saddlebags to leave. No doubt, Kate never missed using her bedpost for a babysitter. As the years went by, the Barry family was finally able to talk about the war in the past tense.

After the war, six more children were added to their already busy household. All the Barry children lived to adulthood, and all married. Andrew died at age sixty-one, and Kate outlived him by fourteen years. Kate and Andrew are buried at Walnut Grove cemetery.

Charles Moore, the patriarch of this heroic family, left the country of his birth and traveled to America to get away from persecution. He left Ireland so he could make his own destiny and not be controlled by a king's edicts. He also left so that he could practice his Presbyterian faith without being persecuted. Therefore, it makes sense that he believed also in the legitimacy of the American Revolution. He passed these values on to his children and practiced them in his community. Kate learned those values as she grew up, and each of her actions as a scout and spy attest to this.

All of Charles and Mary's children were involved in the war and in the rebuilding afterwards. Each of their daughters married Revolutionary War soldiers. The Moore sons became actively involved in both their community and their new country. Thomas Moore was a soldier in the Revolutionary War, a Major-General in the War of 1812, and he served several years in the U.S. Congress. Dr. Andrew Barry Moore, Kate's younger brother, was the first physician in Spartanburg County.

Reading about the war in South Carolina shows that everyone was involved, whether they marched against troops or not. There is no choice when battles are fought in your own backyard. We should not forget the bravery, perseverance, and sacrifice of Kate Moore Barry.

To walk where Kate walked and to visit her girlhood home, you will want to visit Walnut Grove Plantation in Moore, South Carolina. As you are welcomed into Kate's world, remember the liberty you enjoy is because of the sacrifices of people like her!

# Acknowledgments

My love for history was caught rather than taught. The women in my family just love a good book and a good story. My grandmother Lulu entertained my brothers and me with many stories about our ancestors. She loved history and always had a story to tell us about anywhere we traveled together. My grandmother Nanna read historical novels all the time, and she passed them on to my mother and me. We would race through our reading of one book so we could start another one.

I am grateful to my parents for always encouraging me to read. Over the several months of writing *Courageous Kate*, they listened after Sunday dinner as I shared yet another chapter. I could always tell by their faces whether the story had grabbed them or not, and they were again always encouraging and excited about what was next.

To Melissa Walker and George Fields for both their time in reading the manuscript as well as their excellent suggestions and comments for keeping order in a time period that was anything but orderly, I sincerely thank you.

Tom Moore Craig, a great, great, great grandson of Charles and Mary Moore, graciously shared his family papers with me, and they clarified many unknowns. Also, the staff in the Kennedy Room at the Spartanburg Country Library answered my endless questions about this early time in Spartanburg County.

My editor, Betsy Teter, saw potential in an unfinished manuscript and guided me step-by-step to a reality that was once only a dream. Thank you for walking with me through this writing process, and thanks for not using a red pen too much!

My heartfelt thanks go also to my friend and development editor, Clare Neely. You have been so positive from the beginning and have made worthy suggestions that made perfect sense. You pushed me repeatedly on adding the details that made the scenes come alive.

For over twenty years, John, you have encouraged me to write and particularly to write a children's book. Thank you for your kind words. Thank you for answering my endless questions about life on a ship, firing a musket, how a grist mill works, and so many others. I will never forget that day when I was grinding corn with that mill stone. You smiled your encouragement rather than laughing. You drove me from one South Carolina Revolutionary War site to another and were excited with me when we found out something new about colonial times. But most of all, thank you for illustrating *Courageous Kate*. My words and thoughts came alive with your pen.

# About Walnut Grove

Walnut Grove Plantation, the restored girlhood home of Kate Moore Barry, is located eight miles southeast of Spartanburg, South Carolina. From Interstate 26 take exit 28 (S.C. Highway 221) toward Spartanburg and follow the signs.

Guided tours are given of the manor house, kitchen and Rocky Springs Academy. The main house has double-shouldered chimneys, clapboard-over-log construction and Queen Anne mantles. Other buildings on the site include a blacksmith's forge, a wheat house, a smoke house, a barn sheltering a Conestoga wagon, a well house and Dr. Andrew Barry Moore's office. The documented collection of antique furnishings and accessories vividly portrays living conditions in Spartanburg County prior to 1805.

In addition to ancient and lovely oaks and walnuts, the grounds include an herb garden centered with a dipping well and the Moore family cemetery, where Kate Barry, as well as other family members, slaves, and Revolutionary War soldiers are buried. The grounds include a nature trail, picnic area, covered pavilion and vegetable gardens.

Every October the Spartanburg County Historical Association hosts Festifall, a two-day, colonial living history festival, on the grounds of Walnut Grove Plantation. Demonstrators in period clothing show pewtersmithing, blacksmithing, weaving, basketry, joinery work and more.

For more information, call the Spartanburg County Historical Association, 596-3501, or email scha@spartanburghistory.org.

Sheila Ingle is a graduate of Converse College and an adjunct instructor at USC Upstate, where she teaches both English and education classes. She is a member of the Kate Barry Chapter of the Daughters of the American Revolution. *Courageous Kate*, her first book, is the result of her love of history and interest in children's literature.

# Words for Understanding: A Glossary

## ~ Chapter 1 ~

**Scots Irish** – a person of Scottish descent born in Ireland
**Religious freedom** – freedom to worship the denomination
   of   your choice without reprisal of any kind
**Public office** – an elected or appointed office to serve
   the people
**Money bag** – a bag to keep money in on your person
**Christ Church** (Philadelphia) – where George and Martha
   Washington, Benjamin Franklin, and others worshipped
**Quakers** – a religious sect that was very strict in their
   teachings
**Philadelphia Gazette** – weekly newspaper published by
   Benjamin Franklin

## ~ Chapter 2 ~

**Great Philadelphia Wagon Road** – colonial road that ran
   from Philadelphia, Pennsylvania, to Augusta, Georgia
**Anson County** – county in North Carolina now called
   Mecklenburg County
**London Coffee House** – where members of the business and
   maritime communities gathered to discuss business
**Puffy roll** – a yeast roll (favorite of Benjamin Franklin)
**Pack horses** – horses uses by merchants to carry large packs
   of goods and supplies
**Iroquois** – an American Indian tribe
**Poor Richard's Almanac** – an almanac published by
**Benjamin Franklin**
**Ben Franklin** – A great American printer, writer, and statesman
**Land grant** – undeveloped land given by George III to
   professional men

## ~ Chapter 3 ~

**Breeches** – short pants worn by boys
**Vest** – a sleeveless jacket worn under a coat
**Sidesaddle** – a saddle that allowed a lady in a dress
    to ride a horse
**Conestoga wagon** – a popular wagon that the pioneers used
**Powder horn** – a container for gunpowder made from
    a bull's horn
**Cooking fire** – a fire kept burning 24 hours a day used
    for cooking food

## ~ Chapter 4 ~

**Spit** – a set of iron rods used to cook over an open fire
    or in a fireplace
**Pudding cap** – cap worn by toddler learning to walk
**Chinking** – packing mud between logs of a log house
**Keeping room** – family room or living space
**Coonskin hat** – fur hat made from raccoon
**Bible box** – portable box to safely keep Bible and
    important papers in
**Goose and Dice** – Colonial board game

## ~ Chapter 5 ~

**Tansy** – herb
**Cistern** – container for water
**Rosemary** – herb
**Smokehouse** – small shelter to cure meat in
**Sampler** – embroidered cloth with scripture, wise sayings,
    and the alphabet
**Lavender** – herb
**Pinafore** – full apron worn to protect clothes
**Mob cap** – plain cap with gathered crown and frill, usually
    made of linen
**Clabber** – sour, curdled milk
**Butter mold** – shaped mold for decorative butter
**Moccasins** –soft shoes, usually made out of doeskin
**Dustless shelves** – shelves that slanted to floor so dust fell off

**Warming pans** – long-handled metal pans filled with hot
   coals placed between sheets for awhile to warm the bed
**Rag rugs** – crocheted rugs made from scrap cloth
**Johnny cakes** – baked cornbread sweetened with molasses
**Sugar cone/cone sugar** – sugar wrapped in green or blue
   cone ready to be cut and used
**Sugar cutter** – sharp cutter used to cut sugar off sugar cone

~ Chapter 6 ~

**Quilting bee** – women gathering together to make a quilt
   and socialize
**Elder** – elected official to help govern Presbyterian
   congregation
**Militia** – volunteer, part time army
**Propriety** – courtesy and politeness in social relationships
**South Carolina Gazette** – early newspaper published in
   Charles Town
**Milliner** – business woman who sold variety of women's
   clothing and accessories
**Tatting** – fancy stitchery made of knots with a shuttle

~ Chapter 7 ~

**Communion wafers** – small, sugar cookies, often
   personalized and sent as gifts
**Split rail fences** – traditional, American fence about
   four feet high used to keep livestock on property
**Grist mill** – where corn and wheat are ground into flour
**Church doll** – small, cloth doll taken to church; wouldn't
   be disruptive if it fell
**Aesop's Fables** – book of stories about animals that
   teach a lesson
**Hornbook** – small ABC book that children learned
   to read from
**New England Primer** – one of first readers, included pictures
**Dunce cap** – cone-shaped cap worn by uninterested scholars

## ~ Chapter 8 ~

**Mounting block** – steps for mounting a horse
**Treaty of Dewitt's Corner** – when Cherokees signed and
    gave up their land in South Carolina on May 20, 1777
**Scotch-hopper** – hopscotch
**Skirmish** – brief/minor battle between small groups
**King George III** – King of England during Revolutionary War
**Tyranny** – government where a single ruler has absolute
    power
**Custom's House** – built in 1771 in Charles Town; place where
    South Carolina declared independence from England
**Council of Safety** – a forerunner of South Carolina state
    government in 1775
**Fife** – archaic member of the flute family

## ~ Chapter 9 ~

**Hannah's Cow Pens** – place where settlers went to buy
    and sell livestock
**Colonel Tarleton** – British officer known for his cruelty
**Continental Troops** – first, regular U.S. Army under command
**of General Geoge Washington**
**Spinning wheel** –a wheel used to make thread out of
    fibrous material
**Loom** – machine crafted to weave cloth
**Whittling** – art of using small knife to fashion small figure
    or object
**Came courtin'** – old-fashioned term for courtship or dating
**Sir Henry Clinton** – British general during America Revolution
**"Long live the King"** – saying used by the British and Tories
    to show support for King George III
**Patriotism** – support and pride for a particular country

## ~ Chapter 10 ~

**Scout** – person sent out to get advance warning of enemy
**Betty lamp** – oldest form of lamp, usually made of tin

## Chapter 11

**Knapsacks** – backpack used to carry all a soldier's clothing and equipment
**Pouches** – cloth bags
**Allegiance** – loyalty or duty owed to individual country
**Ambush** – secret, planned attack that surprised one's enemies

~ Chapter 12 ~

**Shortbread** – rich, thick, butter cookie that is crunchy
**Millstone** – pair of heavy stones that rotate against each other to grind grain

~ Chapter 13 ~

**Kindling** – small pieces of wood used to start a fire
**Major General Nathaniel Greene** – commander of Southern campaign
**General Daniel Morgan** – commander of Continentals and militia at the Battle of Cowpens
**Colonel Andrew Pickens** – Scots-Irish commander of militia from Abbeville County, South Carolina

# Bibliography

Babits, Lawrence E. *Cowpens Battlefield: A Walking Guide*.
   Johnson City, Tennessee: The Overmountain Press, 1993.
Bodie, Idella. *The Old Wagoner*. Orangeburg: Sandlapper
   Publishing Co., 2002.
— *Historic Walnut Grove Plantation*, 1765. Up Country
   Heritage. Spartanburg County South Carolina.
Edgar, Walter. *Partisans and Redcoats*. New York: Perennial,
   2001.
Fleming, Thomas J. *Cowpens*. United States: National Park
   Services Division Of Publications, 1988.
Foster, Vernon and Walter S. Montgomery, Sr., eds.
   *Spartanburg: Facts, Reminiscences, Folklore*. Spartanburg:
   The Reprint Co., 1998.
Fryar, Jack E., Jr. ed.  Benson J. *Lossing's Pictorial Field-Book
   of the Revolution in the Carolina & Georgia*. Wilmington:
   Dram Tree Books, 2005.
Hope, Wes. *Spartanburg Area in the American Revolution*.
   Spartanburg: Kinko's, 2002.
Hiatt, John. *Historic Resource Study Part 1: The Battle of
   Musgrove's Mill*. Columbia: South Carolina State Park
   Service, 2000.
Landrum, Dr. J. B. O. *History of Spartanburg County*. Atlanta,
   Georgia: The Franklin Printing and Publishing Company,
   1900.
McCrady, Edward. *The History of S. C. in the Revolution 1775
   1780*. New York: Russell & Russell, 1901.
McWhorter, Lottie and Lou Ann Melton, eds. *Mary (Barry) 1795
   and William Barry Henderson (1787-1863)*. Baltimore:
   Gatway Press, Inc., 1987.
Moore, Colonel T. J. *Reminisces of Nazareth Church Cemetery
   and Family Burial Grounds*. Spartanburg: Band and White
   Printing, 1903.
Palmer, B. M. *An Address at the One Hundreth Anniversary of
   the Organization of the Nazareth Church and Congregation*

*in Spartanburg, S. C.* Richmond: Shepperson & Co. Printers, 1872.

Racine, Philip. N. *Seeing Spartanburg, a History in Images*. Spartanburg: Hub City Writers Project, 1999.

Roberts, Kenneth. *The Battle of Cowpens: The Great Morale Builder*. New York: Doubleday & Company, Inc., 1958.

Scheer, George F. and Hugh F. Rankin. *Rebels and Redcoats*. New York: World Publishing Company, 1957.

Spartanburg Unit of the Writers Program of the Work Projects Administration in the State of S.C. *A History of Spartanburg County*. Spartanburg: The Reprint Co., 1976.

Spruill, Julia Cherry. *Women's Life and Work in the Southern Colonies*. New York: W. W. Norton & Co., 1972.

Steedman, Marguerite Couterrier. *The S. C. Colony*. London: Crowell-Collier Press, 1970.

Swager, Christine R. *Come to the Cowpens!* Spartanburg: Hub City Writers Project, 2002.

Thomas, Sam. *The Dye is Cast: The Scots-Irish and Revolution in the Carolina Back Country*. Columbia: The Palmetto Conservation Foundation.

Thompson, Ernest Trice. *Presbyterians in the South*. Volume 1. Richmond: John Knox Press, 1963.

Babits, Lawrence E. *A Devil of a Whipping: The Battle of Cowpens*. Chapel Hill: The University of N. C. Press, 1998.

Morrill, Dan L. *Southern Campaigns of the American Revolution*. Baltimore: The Nautical & Aviation Publishing Co. of America, 1993.

Magill, Arthur. *Battle of the Cowpens*. Greenville: The Reedy River Press, Inc., 1980.

White, Katherine. *The King's Mountain Men*. Baltimore: Genealogical Publishing Co., 1966.

The Hub City Writers Project is a non-profit organization whose mission is to foster a sense of community through the literary arts. We do this by publishing books from and about our community; encouraging, mentoring, and advancing the careers of local writers; and seeking to make Spartanburg a center for the literary arts.

Our metaphor of organization purposely looks backward to the nineteenth century when Spartanburg was known as the "hub city," a place where railroads converged and departed.

At the beginning of the twenty-first century, Spartanburg has become a literary hub of South Carolina with an active and nationally celebrated core group of poets, fiction writers, and essayists. We celebrate these writers—and the ones not yet discovered—as one of our community's greatest assets. William R. Ferris, former director of the Center for the Study of Southern Cultures, says of the emergng South, "Our culture is our greatest resource. We can shape an economic base ... And it won't be an investment that will disappear."

Printed in the USA
CPSIA information can be obtained
at www.ICGtesting.com
JSHW020752300124
56338JS00001B/2

9 781891 885525